A Border Runs Through It

Plate IX. Vol. V. Part II.
page 192.

age by Land to
IFORNIA
er it by ye Rev Fath.
us Francis Kino Iesut
m of Years 1698 & 1701

Turquesos 1701

A Large Mountain reaching to the River Hila

Moqui

Apaches

R. Bleue

Rio Azul

NEW MEXICO

Achedomas

Rio colorado ó del Norte

S. Mathieu de Scorvide

Casa grande R. de Hila ou de le Hila

S. Fer.

S. Victor

S. Philips

Thadé de Batqui

S. S. Eugene

S. Pantele

Dionysio 1700

S. Simon de Viadaibuss

S. Jacque

S. Pierre S. Mathias

la Sota

Tutomagodag. de Suefani

S. Angelo

S. Ca therine

baip

Rosario

S. Auaustin

S. M.

S. Paulo 1699

Cocomaricopas

la Tinara

S. Francois

S. Boniface

S. Cosne

Xavier

Sauveur

Yumas

Agua escondida

Aguage de la Luna

la Merced

S. Raphael

S. Seraphin

S. Francois du Bac

S. Gaetan

Bagiopas

Carizal

S. Marcel

S. Louis de Bacapa

PIMERIA

Reyes

Guebari

S. Louis

S. Marie

S. Lazare

Quaquimas

Sierra Azul M. Bleue

Medanos 3 Ojitos M. de S. Claire 1698

Batequi

S. Eulalie

Susanic

Aquimuri

Cocospara

Remedios

Bachan

Chi

Sierra Nevada

S. Edouard de Baipia

Tubutuma

Adid

Himeris

Tupo

S. Ignace

Dolores

Arisse

Cucurpa

Onaguca

Montagne couverte de neige

S. Marc

S. Mathiu

R. de S. Ignace

Sobas

Concention del Tubcoa

S. Antoine de Uquitoa

S. Diegue de Pitqui

Magdalena

Tacapa

Onodepa

Nacameri

Populo

S. Xavier

Sonora

Ures

Alames

S. Jean

P. de S. Sabine

Naaeyno

Topoquis

Sobas

Angelos

Ulres

S. Xavier

S. Miguel

THE SEA OF

I. S. Augustin

Bage de S. Jean Baptiste

R. de Sonora

Tecorina

Comeripa

Tecorim

Zuaq

S. Rosalie

les Verges

Isles de Sel

C. de S. Xavier

R. Hiaque

Gunimas

Hiaquin

Belen

Bacum

Potam

Torem

Bicam

NEW

MAYO

S. Antoino

Sag. 74

P. de S. Antoin

R. de Usya

P. des Salines

Nabzyor

H. chofon

S. Creus

B. de S. Christophe

R. du Detm.

Guimies

S. Jean de Londo

S. Bruno Coronados

B. S. Luc

les Verges

S. Isidry

Carmen

Farellon

Thebaida

Nicholas

Reyes

Nochebuena

Loreto

S. Etienne

S. Jean

Concho

S. Xavier de Biuando

Gigante

B. du Delen.

Santiago

S. Jacque

Rio de S. Thomas

Edües

Port de Ganganta

Port de Malanzas

B. du Sables

les S. S. Innocens

THE SOUTH SEA
discovered 1686

Yodivineggo

THE SEA OF CALIFORNIA

OF CALIFORNIA

PT OF CALIFORNIA

A Border Runs Through It

Journeys in Regional History and Folklore

BY JIM GRIFFITH

ILLUSTRATIONS BY
DAVID FITZSIMMONS

RIO NUEVO
PUBLISHERS

Tucson, Arizona

Rio Nuevo Publishers®
P.O. Box 5250
Tucson, AZ 85703-0250
(520) 623-9558, www.rionuevo.com

Book design: Karen Schober Book Design.
Jacket design: David Jenney.

Printed in the United States of America.

10 9 8 7 6 5 4 3 2 1

Library of Congress Cataloging-in-Publication Data

Griffith, James S.
  A border runs through it : journeys in regional history and folklore / by Jim Griffith.
    p. cm.
  Includes bibliographical references.
  ISBN-13: 978-1-933855-62-2 (hardcover : alk. paper)
  ISBN-10: 1-933855-62-2 (hardcover : alk. paper)
1. Folklore--Pimería Alta (Mexico and Ariz.) 2. Pimería Alta (Mexico and Ariz.)--History. 3. Pimería Alta (Mexico and Ariz.)--Folklore. 4. Pimería Alta (Mexico and Ariz.)--Social life and customs. I. Title.
  GR115.5.P56G75 2011
  398.209789--dc23

                          2011030160

Contents

INTRODUCTION 1

———

CHAPTER ONE: TREKKING THROUGH TUCSON 7

CHAPTER TWO: THE TREK CONTINUES, WITH DIGRESSIONS AND A CALENDAR 33

CHAPTER THREE: PILGRIMAGE PATHS 51

CHAPTER FOUR: DESERT WANDERINGS 77

CHAPTER FIVE: RIDING THE GRUB TRAIL 93

———

EPILOGUE: BUT WE CAN'T STOP NOW 105

AFTERWORD 112

ACKNOWLEDGMENTS 115

BIBLIOGRAPHY 116

INDEX 120

ABOUT THE AUTHOR / ABOUT THE ILLUSTRATOR 122

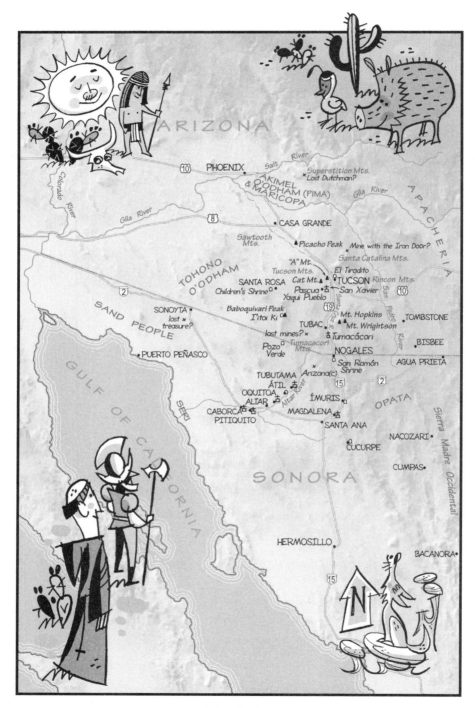

Pimería Alta.

Introduction

THIS BOOK WAS INSPIRED BY the warm reception given to my "Southern Arizona Traditions" series which ran in the 1980s and 90s on Tucson's KUAT-TV *Arizona Illustrated* program. A series of short, three-to-five-minute on-site introductions to various aspects of our region's folklore and traditional cultures, it gained a faithful following among long-term Anglo and Mexican American residents, as well as among recent arrivals to the desert. Realizing that a similarly themed book might also stir public interest, Susan Lowell of Rio Nuevo Publishers suggested that I turn the series into a book. This is the result.

There are some differences between the TV shows and the written version. The TV series was ad-libbed in front of the camera; I have substituted a series of short, original essays on many of the same topics. But not all, however. The traditional visual arts and music of Southern Arizona's Mexicano population have been adequately dealt with in my book, *Hecho A Mano,* so I have limited myself for the most part to places, beliefs, legends, and food. Because I have not had to keep each topic down to a short time slot, I have expanded on some of the subjects, run other topics together, and digressed freely. This last is perhaps the most important difference: digression being one of the spices of life, we'll go about our journeying somewhat the way my dogs take a walk in the desert, dashing off to investigate strange sights, smells, and rumors, and always alert to the possibility of food. After all, I have always suspected that dogs have more fun than arrows or bullets, which do as they are told and go straight to the mark.

But before we get started, a little explanation is in order. I arrived in Tucson in January 1956 to attend the University of Arizona and learn to become an archaeologist. After a few years, I learned that cultural anthropologists studied much the same stuff, but without the heavy work of digging. Finally, it became clear that folklorists had even more fun, so I've defined myself as a folklorist since 1970. Folklorists study the informal, traditional, creative aspects of human cultural behavior—the songs, the art, the stories, the beliefs that serve to give us our identity. In the Great Store of human activity, many of us feel that we work in the Toy Department.

So much for the academic side of things. When I first came to Tucson, I was fascinated by what you might call the classic Southwest—the Four Corners region, home of the Navajo and Hopi, land of spectacular ancient ruins and gorgeous rugs and silver. Every chance I got, my vacation needle pointed north. But slowly I realized that I was living in a region where many of the needles pointed south. I saw—and was deeply moved by—the Yaqui Easter ceremony. I visited mission churches in Sonora, and organized a museum exhibit about the traditional arts of northwest Mexico. Southern Arizona—and northwest Mexico—is where I've been working and learning ever since.

The "Pimería Alta" is the name given by the Spaniards to the northern portion of the lands occupied by the people they called "Pimas," and who called themselves variations on "O'odham," which means "The People." I'll talk about those names a little later. The Pimería Alta stretches from the San Pedro Valley west almost as far as the Colorado River, and from the Salt River Basin south to around Santa Ana, Sonora. This book represents my very personal explorations of this territory over the past forty-five years. There is plenty more to say about the region, its people, history, and customs. This is just a beginning.

People have been living in this region for a long time. Down near present-day Naco, they hunted mammoths around 11,000 B.C. They killed and butchered those huge beasts using stone tools. And I suspect they worked hard to get that meal, and ate well when they were successful. About six thousand years later, folks were growing corn in the Santa Cruz Valley, near present-day Marana. And later still, the Hohokam people operated huge and complex irrigation systems in present-day Maricopa County. The relationship between these ancient peoples and today's native populations is still unclear. For a person interested in continuity, therefore, the best starting place for the stories of this region is the late seventeenth century, when Father Eusebio Francisco Kino rode west out of the mission village of Cucurpe in present-day Sonora and began to visit the O'odham. He ushered in tremendous changes in the human life of our region, changes that continue to this day. More changes followed the Gadsden Purchase of 1854, and continued through the nineteenth century and up to the present day.

The Arizona of a hundred years ago had a diverse and cosmopolitan population of men and women who enriched our local scene with their cultural traditions. One way to get a handle on this fact is to stroll through some of our older cemeteries, especially in the mining camps. You'll find Mexican names, of course, but also Serbs, Croats, and Montenegrins, especially in the Globe–Miami area and in Bisbee. You'll find Italians up north in Jerome. A little later on, you'll find Chinese names and inscriptions in Chinese, especially in the larger, more stable, and tolerant towns. In the Mesa cemetery, you'll find quite a few gravestones erected for Englishmen—RAF pilots who crashed while over here for training during World War II.

It's not just ethnicity that crops up in our cemeteries. Occupation is often celebrated in one way or another. In Bisbee, old drill bits are often used as armatures for concrete fenceposts. One old prospector in Arivaca is memorialized with a reproduction of a claim monument. His nickname was "Klondyke." Cowboy graves may have fences and crosses made of horseshoes. Towards the end of the twentieth century, sandblasting technology allowed gravestones to be illustrated with pictures of cars, motorcycles, horses, and other motifs—all telling something about the occupants of the graves. Finally, it is easy to distinguish the prominent families in any community, as they could afford to order metal markers from foundries back East, mostly, it seems, in Missouri and Ohio. These often elaborate confections would arrive by train in pieces, and be assembled on the spot.

Religion also comes to the fore in our cemeteries. Mormon tombstones often have genealogies on them, or representations of one or another of the temples. Catholic cemeteries, and especially Mexican Catholic cemeteries, are filled with representations of Christ, the Virgin, and various saints. This was forcibly brought home to me on my first visit to the Evergreen Cemetery on Oracle Road in Tucson. I was walking among the carefully aligned, orderly gravestones of the Protestant cemetery and happened to glance north towards the Catholic section. The place was filled with statues of the Virgin, of angels blowing trumpets, of saints, all clustered together in a wonderful confusion of activity. My eyes and my interest immediately leaped the barrier, and I have been living in that highly visual world of images ever since. Loveliest of all, perhaps, are the small-town Mexican cemeteries on both sides of the border, where local craftspeople have embellished the grave markers. I have seen crosses of plumber's pipe, bearing finials recycled from china and brass doorknobs or old oilcans. I have seen statues of saints inside niches made from half-buried bathtubs. I have seen earthen grave mounds outlined by beer or tequila bottles half buried in the ground, neck down. And on and on.

In these ways and others, the living make statements about their dead and about their values. People accustomed to the rather talkative epitaphs "back East" will not find many such in Arizona. One, down in Tombstone's "new" cemetery (started in the 1880s), is the best of a small lot:

Here lies Mac, dead and in his grave.
No more liquor will he crave.
But while he lived, it can be wrote
Many a quart went down his throat.

That this wild diversity of cultural origin and expression has only intensified in the twenty-first century may be seen if one visits Tucson Meet Yourself, an annual folklife festival held each October in El Presidio Park in downtown Tucson. Here one encounters many members of the ethnic groups that make up the community, performing their traditional music and dance, selling traditional foods, and demonstrating traditional arts. From the longest-term residents—the Tohono O'odham—right up to recent refugees from Somalia and Afghanistan, people from all over the world now share our desert with us. And so Tucson Meet Yourself at various times has presented a Chinese orchestra, Carpathian dancers, Ukrainian Easter egg decorators, and food prepared by Lebanese, Indian, Polish, Greek, Korean, and Costa Rican cooks. And all these folks are Tucson residents, and all add to the flavors, sounds, and tastes of today's Pimería Alta.

There is another side to this same coin, of course. Such diversity implies a high rate of immigration, and indeed, at any time over the past thirty years, about one third of the residents of Pima County have lived here for less than five years. As I will try to show in this book, our region does have its own cultural traditions. Providing ways for all these recent arrivals to find out about these traditions, this regional identity, has been my life's work. And, as the human tsunami continues to wash into our area, it's work that must continue. And that is the real reason for this book. It is, if you will, a map, complete with instructions, to the cultural treasures that lie buried, often just below the surface or in plain sight, in this fascinating country. As is the case with many older maps, this one has been visually embellished with illustrations and motifs, large and small. These come from the hand and mind of *Arizona Daily Star* cartoonist David Fitzsimmons, best known simply as "Fitz." And now the treasure hunt is ready to begin.

Oh, yes—one confession. We folklorists claim to tell everything just as we heard it—we are reporters, not creators of folklore. I have broken this rule in the case of three tall tales, or "windies." I have told suckers about sand trout and stick lizards for years, and have added my details to the common stock. And I wrote 'em like I tell 'em.

CHAPTER ONE

Trekking through Tucson

LET'S BEGIN OUR VIRTUAL JOURNEY where I am writing this, in Tucson, Arizona. First, we'll look at the city's name, which isn't pronounced the way it's spelled. Then we'll wander through a maze of legends, places, people, art forms, and foods that are associated in one way or another with our city.

PLACE NAMES

Many of you may have had the same experience I have: I answer the phone, only to find a fund solicitor calling long distance, referring to a place he calls "Tukson." (On one memorable occasion, the phrase was "right here in Tukson.") That's my signal to hang up the phone. But why the gap between the written and spoken names? Here's the story.

Before any Europeans came to this place, there was an O'odham village on the west bank of the Santa Cruz (Spanish name) River, at the foot of what we now call "'A' Mountain," but which, before it was decorated by University of Arizona students in November of 1915, following a pair of football victories over Pomona College, was called "Sentinel Peak." The O'odham name for the hill was purely descriptive: "Schuk Doag" or "Black Mountain." The village was called "Schuk Shon," or "at the black base." In 1776 a Spanish *presidio* or cavalry outpost across the river was called "Tucsón," as close as the Spanish tongue could come to the O'odham original. English-speaking arrivals seemed to retain this pronunciation, as "Tukson" and "Tuxon" appear in Civil War diaries. The current pronunciation of "Toosahn" may well have come in around the 1880s after the railroad connected us with the rest of the country, and pressures for statehood and "Americanization" of this Mexican territory mounted. A final shift took place around the 1940s and 50s, when stressing the second syllable of the city's name, as in "Tucsón," no longer became an option.

The origin of "Arizona" is another story. The name comes from a ranch in what is now northern Sonora, some 20 miles southwest of present-day Nogales, near the site of a fabulous discovery of silver in 1736. (The original name is often given as "Arizonac," the result of an early and much-quoted map. Contemporary accounts, however, all call it "Arizona.")

So now the question remains of what "Arizona" means. It is certainly not a garbling of the Spanish word for "dry zone"—the place gets good annual rainfall. Probably not from the O'odham, either, as there was no O'odham village in the area. The mostly likely explanation so far is that "Arizona" is actually "Aritz Onah," a Basque phrase meaning "good oak tree." Bernardo de Urrea, owner of the Arizona Ranch in the 1730s, was himself a Basque, like many other Sonoran pioneers. There are oak trees in the valley where the rancho Arizona was (and still is). For further reading on this fascinating topic, see Don Garate's *Journal of Arizona History* articles in the bibliography.

The name was first proposed for a new territory comprising the western part of New Mexico in 1854 by the New Mexico Territorial legislature. Other possibilities that were floated in that general time frame were "Pimeria" and "Gadsdonia." However, "Arizona" won.

Without going too far into details, here are some generalizations about the naming of places in this region. The O'odham tend to use descriptive names, like "Black Mountain"—there are a lot of hills by that name in southern Arizona. Spaniards used descriptives as well: "la Ciénaga"—"the marsh," or "el Rincón"—"the corner." They also used saints' names like "Santa Catalina" or "Santa Rita." These not only labeled the land but placed it under the protection of a specific saint, thus in a sense Christianizing it. Often the name was that of the saint on or near whose day the name was bestowed. When the English-speaking Americans came along, we tended to name features after other Americans, either historic figures or local folks. Mt. Hopkins, for example, was named after a mining engineer who was killed by Apaches in 1865, while Mt. Wrightson owes its name to a mine manager who suffered a similar fate in 1861. Mining in that period was a pretty dangerous occupation, taking place as it usually did in isolated areas. Finally, in the twentieth century, real estate developers looked for names that would sell. Often the principle here has been one of some sort of romantic association. There's a lot of ersatz Spanish (Rancho Sin Vacas, Camino de Michael) scattered over our maps. And, of course, there are the place names where Spanish and English say the same thing: the Rillito River, Picacho Peak, and my favorite of all, Table Mesa north of Phoenix. The easiest way to reveal this particular brand of silliness would be to translate both words in each name, which leaves us "Little River Rillito," "Peak Picacho," and "Mesa Table." More recently, there seems to be a belief that adding an extra "e" to words such as "Pointe" gives an aura of exclusivity and increases the sum folks might pay for house lots. Why a phony French spelling should induce people to pay more for their house lot is unclear, but it seems to work.

While we are on the subject of names, let's take a look at Tucson's barrios. *Barrio* as it is used here simply means "neighborhood," or as my friend Alfredo Gonzales has it, " 'barrio' means 'home.' " In fact there is an area in midtown Tucson, settled by younger, professional-class Mexican Americans called "Barrio Volvo." Many non-Hispanics, however, use the word incorrectly to signify a sort of Mexican ghetto. And recently, a fairly exclusive development called "Barrio Tubac" has come into existence near the town of that name. Different groups use the same words to mean different things.

But the majority of Tucson's barrios are primarily Mexican neighborhoods on the west, south, and southwest sides of town. They are not always marked on maps, and their boundaries can be fluid, but the people who live there know where they are and what their names are.

For Tucson's barrios are named: there is Barrio Menlo Park just west of the river, and Barrio Hollywood to the north of that. Further north still is Barrio Sobaco—"Armpit Barrio"—named possibly because of the curvature of the streets, and possibly as an insult on the part of residents of a neighboring barrio. And far to the south of South Tucson, where the streets have names like Nebraska and Ohio, is "Barrio States." My all-time favorite? A tiny barrio just south of Congress and east of Grande, whose official name is Barrio Sin Nombre ("The Nameless Barrio"). As of August 2009, the Barrio Sin Nombre Neighborhood Association has officially changed its name to "Barrio San Agustín," after Tucson's patron saint. A nice idea—let's see if it sticks.

Just to make things a little more complicated, different groups of people may have different names for the same place. Back in the 1940s and 50s, there were Mexican Americans all over the Southwest who self-identified as *pachucos*. Pachucos were young, wore zoot suits, occasionally moved on the wrong side of the law, and spoke their own argot. Pachuco was a bit more than Border Spanish or "Spanglish"—it has its own words and its own style. And its own slang place names. El Paso was "el Chuco," Tucson was "la Tusa," Los Angeles "el Los," and California "el Califas." And one still occasionally hears these place names today.

Back in the 1980s, I was given another set of place names—those used when giving instructions to illegal immigrants for the desert trek north from near Sasabe up to Picacho Peak. The names were purely descriptive, and required no local knowledge to understand. First one steered for el Tambor ("the Drum," a perfectly good identifier for Baboquivari Mountain). From el Tambor, one headed for el Serrucho or "the Saw." The Sawtooth Mountains lie to the northeast of the Altar Valley. From el Serrucho it was a clear walk to el Picacho (Picacho Peak) and farming country. Beyond that, one can reach Phoenix and indeed all of the United States.

While we are on the subject of specialized names for places, let's wind up on a lighter note. I know some Mexican American residents of Tumacácori in the upper Santa Cruz Valley who refer to the nearby town of Tubac as "Dos P'atras" which, translated into English, is "Two Back."

Having worked our way down to a detailed discussion of specialized names, let's flip back to the big picture—the region I'm writing about is called the "Pimería Alta." Missionaries bestowed this name when they realized the folks into whose country they were moving had a language and culture similar to other folks to the south whom they called "Pimas." (Remnants of this southern Pima population still live in Yécora and Maicoba, up in the Sierra Madre mountains on the Sonora–Chihuahua border.)

But nothing is simple, as the people up here whom the Spaniards called "Pimas" have always called themselves "O'odham," which means "People." "Pima" seems to have come from an O'odham word meaning "I don't know." One can, if one so desires, imagine a Spaniard on his horse questioning an O'odham in Spanish: "What are your people called? Who is your ruler?" and so forth. The Indian replies, in his own language: "I don't know what you're talking about." And the Spaniard carefully writes it down. Fanciful, but fun.

There are three good books on Arizona's place names, two by Byrd Howell Granger and one by Will C. Barnes, listed in the bibliography, should you wish to delve deeper into this subject.

El Tejano

This story takes us back into the third quarter of the nineteenth century, when the Mexican community pronounced "Tuksón" was starting to grow into the "American" city of Tucson. It concerns a stage robber whose name has been lost to the written record (and who may or may not have actually existed). Northwest Mexico is still a land of nicknames, and so it's fitting that this bad man is remembered only by his *apodo* or nickname of "El Tejano"— "The Texan." While you won't find him in contemporary newspapers, he is still very real in the stories of older Mexicanos in Pima County. He preyed on the stagecoaches that transported pay chests to outlying mining communities, and his success in this game was attributed by some to the fact that he had an inside contact with the stage company. The late Pete Castillo of Marana told me the following story about him: Nobody could catch El Tejano, although some folks had their suspicions as to who he was. Finally the stage company hired a really sharp detective from California. The detective went to the stage stop at El Picacho (Picacho Peak), where the suspect's wife was employed, and inquired after her husband, only to be told that he wasn't there. "Why of course," said the detective. "I just saw him in Phoenix. He was at the gambling tables, drinking and having a wonderful time with some of the ladies there." "Why, that no-good so-and-so!" exclaimed the wife. "He said he was going to rob a stage!" Oops!

Tradition has it that El Tejano was finally killed by a shotgun blast on el Cerro del Gato or Cat Mountain, just west of Tucson and north of what is now Ajo Way. When his corpse was laid out by the courthouse, hundreds of people filed by to see him. But his ghost has been seen well into the mid-twentieth century, riding a horse across the desert (and raising no dust in doing so), or heard at midnight, leading his horse down to the river to drink water that hasn't flowed there for fifty years.

End of the story? Not quite. For El Tejano is said to have buried his treasure, and it has never been found. Perhaps it's on Cat Mountain, perhaps elsewhere in the Tucson Mountains, perhaps somewhere else entirely. Wherever it is, El Tejano still guards it. If you are lucky enough (or otherwise) to find the treasure, you'll hear a voice saying "*Todo o nada*"—"Everything or nothing at all." The voice is El Tejano's, and this is its message: If you leave the site with only some of the money (and there's too much to carry away at one time) you will die. If you walk off empty-handed, meaning to come back with a means of carrying off all the treasure, you'll never find the site again. I've been told circumstantial stories, complete with names, of men who have removed bits of El Tejano's gold and died before they could return for the rest.

Was there a real El Tejano? Nobody knows. Folklorist Joyce Gibson Roach, who reported on the legend cycle in the 1960s, suggested that at least parts of his story were based on the career of one William Brazelton, who originally hailed from Missouri. Arriving in Arizona around 1875, he robbed stages from near the Mexican border north to Prescott. He worked in a livery stable in Tucson, and was killed in 1878.

Stage robbers indeed plied their trade in southern Arizona and northern Sonora, and left evidence behind them. Several years ago, near the Sonoran border town of Sonoyta, a bulldozer clearing ground for a new road cut into a cache of coins. All were new-looking silver one-peso pieces, dated between 1890 and 1900. There had been mines nearby in those days, and the logical explanation for the cache is that it represented the loot from a payroll robbery, buried in its original sack, which then rotted away.

The entire town turned out to gather the coins, of course. As the story goes, at the height of their frenzy, an elderly Indian man walked by, watched the activity for a while, and said, "That's the silver. The gold is over there," pointing with his chin. That gold, if it ever existed, was never found, and the site of the cache is now on a military reservation.

Just another treasure story from this land of great stories. A little late for El Tejano's treasure, of course, but proof that loot has not only been buried, but found again. And, of course, there are folks who believe that because El Tejano's treasure hasn't been found, that must mean that it's still there. For others such as myself, the story itself, along with all the other stories like it, is the treasure.

A good introduction to El Tejano is "The Legends of El Tejano, The Texan Who Never Was," by Joyce Gibson Roach.

EL TIRADITO

The El Minuto Cafe occupies the southwest corner of Cushing Street and Main Avenue, just south of the Convention Center parking lot. Directly south of the restaurant is a parking lot, and directly south of this is another vacant lot. This is the site of El Tiradito, or the Wishing Shrine, Tucson's informal Place of Petitions. The shrine itself is unimpressive at first glance: a vacant lot backed by an adobe wall with a central niche, some metal candleholders, and a large number of "six-day" votive candles in glass jars, some lit, others burned out.

Then one notices that the ground in front of the wall is stained dark, apparently from years of candle grease deposits. In my forty years of visiting the shrine, I have only once seen anybody praying there. However, there have been lit candles on every visit.

This is where many Tucsonans come to plug into some source of power that they feel has been denied them. It may be a healing power, or the power to get out of jail, or, as one boy told a folklorist many years ago, the power to get a new car, or pass into fourth grade. Some come and light a candle to ensure a successful hunting trip, or a prize in a dog show. The site is visited by people from many of Tucson's cultures and walks of life. It is our Wishing Shrine.

If you look around, you will find an official historic marker telling you that this is the "only shrine in the United States dedicated to the soul of a sinner buried in unconsecrated ground." It further outlines the City of Tucson's "official legend and story" concerning the site: a young sheepherder named Juan Oliveros, who lived on a ranch out of town, was carrying on an impassioned affair with his mother-in-law. One day the husband/father-in-law surprised the guilty couple in their adulterous love, killed Juan with his axe, and then fled for Mexico. Juan was buried where he fell.

It's a great story. However, there are no known contemporary accounts of this event, and there exist in the University of Arizona Library's Folklore Archive over twenty other, mutually exclusive, stories. They range from detailed, romantic narratives to the story of a man who was walking past a bar and was felled by a stray bullet. In a case such as this, you pretty much pays your money and takes your choice. Finally, if anyone was ever "buried on the spot" (a common theme to the stories) there is no proof of that either. The shrine has been moved at least once, and there's a good chance that in its original form it was not a grave at all, but a cross to mark the site of a sudden death—a common Mexican practice that I'll discuss later on in the book.

El Tiradito (the name means "the little cast-away one") enters Tucson's written historical record in the April 1, 1893, issue of the *Arizona Star*, in a small, untitled paragraph that describes an improvised shrine in downtown Tucson. On the same spot, "many years" before, a Mexican had been murdered.

The article mentions unnamed "superstitions" connected with the site. In 1909 an actor named George Berrell visited the shrine and saw many candles burning. Assuming that each candle represented a separate prayer, it is safe to say that the site was in use by the public.

Later on, in the 1920s, the shrine was moved as a result of a road-widening project and relocated to its present site, on land donated to the City of Tucson by a local Mexican American pioneer. By 1927 the Tucson City Council had selected the "official legend and story" from among the many legends that were in circulation. Why this sudden attention on the part of the city establishment? I suspect that, with the arrival of the railroad in 1880 when Tucson was connected with the rest of the United States, and with Arizona's finally gaining statehood in 1912, Mexican culture was slowly moving in the eyes of the Anglo establishment from an embarrassment to a marketable commodity. People from out of town would actually visit the site and enjoy the stories. (And they still do—the day before I wrote this, there was a tour bus parked in front of El Tiradito!)

But the story continues. In the 1960s, a sizeable chunk of what had been nineteenth-century Mexican Tucson was swallowed up by a huge "urban renewal" project. A few years later, in 1971, the Butterfield Parkway was planned to pass through several of the remaining downtown barrios. This time the city's Mexican American residents decided to "fight City Hall"... and won! One of their tactics was to get El Tiradito on the National Register of Historic Places—thus the sign I described all those paragraphs ago. The Butterfield never happened, and El Tiradito is still there—another case in which folks lacking power went to the site to get what they needed.

So El Tiradito has persisted as an active presence in Tucson for over a century. It is still a place of petitions, but today it is much more. It is a destination, not just for commercial tours but for private individuals wanting to show their visitors something significant about Tucson. Folklorists and journalists write about it every few years. In a sense, this unprepossessing site has become a sort of symbol of Tucson.

A more thorough discussion of El Tiradito may be found in Chapter 4 of my book, *A Shared Space: Folklife in the Arizona-Sonora Borderlands.*

Mission San Xavier del Bac

The Pimería Alta is full of time machines—places or occasions through which one can enter, if ever so briefly, a previous period in history. Perhaps the best-known and most elaborate of these is the mission church of San Xavier del Bac, about twelve miles south of Tucson, just west of I-19. A village has stood on this site since time immemorial. Following O'odham custom, the place was called "Bac," which meant that at this place, the river water ran on the surface. (Languages change over the years, and the "b" in "Bac" has softened into a "w" sound—Wa:k. The colon means that the "a" sound has stretched out slightly—"Waak.") The pioneering Jesuit missionary Father Eusebio Francisco Kino first visited here in 1692, established a mission program, and had plans for building a church, which never came to fruition. It was the 1750s before a simple adobe hall church was constructed, with a door at one end and an altar at the other.

Then in 1767, as a result of political conflicts in Europe, all the Jesuits—Father Kino's order—were expelled from the Spanish colonies and replaced a year later by Franciscans. It was they who built the elaborate church we see today. And the old church? It was dismantled and moved, piece by piece, to the east side of the new one, where it was recycled into the *convento* wing that stands there today. The new church was dedicated in 1797.

And there it has stood 'til the present—slowly deteriorating, to be sure, but always patched up before total disaster had a chance to strike. The most recent round of "patching-up" started in the 1990s. It is still going on as I write this and will eventually involve the stripping of the old plaster from all the exterior surfaces, the replacement of whatever bricks need it, and the application of new lime plaster. To make the plaster more water-repellent, prickly pear juice is added to the mixture just as it was 200 years ago. As one conservator remarked, low-tech problems demand low-tech solutions.

The interior with its statues and painting has already been cleaned and stabilized, and the old church's colors glow more brightly than they have for well over a century. How do you clean a 200-year-old mural? It's simple, but not easy. First you make sure the paint doesn't peel away from the wall. With a hypodermic needle, you inject some sort of adhesive material between the brick wall and the rough coat of plaster, between the rough coat and the finish coat, and between the finish coat and the layer of paint. Then, to clean the mural of centuries of smoke and grime, you hold a sheet of rice paper against the painted surface, and pat it with a moistened sponge. The liquid enters the paint and puts the dirt into solution. The dirt rises to the surface of the paint, and when you lift the paper off, the dirt lifts off as well. Of course, it helps to know what you're doing.

By the way, San Xavier presents us with the finest example of the baroque style of architecture in our border region. This style, which still influences how contemporary Mexicans and Mexican Americans organize things and events, deserves a little attention before we go any farther. Its principles include implied motion, dramatic contrasts between light and shadow, richness of surface decoration and richness of colors, and a certain ambiguity. The motion is easy to see—there really aren't many simple straight lines in the church. Cornices zig in and zag out. Columns turn into complex confections of rectangles, pyramids, and lozenges. Most of the statues seem to have been caught in the midst of some sort of activity. Little space is left unpainted or uncarved, and there is gold and silver leaf enough to satisfy anyone. As for the ambiguity, look at the fake doors painted in the nave and the sanctuary, the plaster carved and painted to look like rocks, or the life-sized statues that can almost fool you into thinking they are real people, about to move.

As long as we travel among Mexican people, we'll see echoes of this baroque style—in the decorations of roadside chapels, in the opulent decorations of low-rider cars, in the richly layered meanings of Tucson's murals. It's with us constantly, and serves as a strong link tying past to present. For an essay on the persistence of the baroque style, see Chapter 8 of *A Shared Space*.

But let's return to our concept of the church as a time machine. When you walk through the door, you find yourself in an almost complete, late-eighteenth century environment. Even more, you find yourself inside a late-eighteenth century rendering of heaven, complete with God the Father (He has red hair and green eyes), and saints, martyrs, and angels, all painted and sculpted on the walls of the church. Especially angels—I personally find it hard to keep track of all the angels; there's always a chance that they come and go.

Who created all this spectacular art? We don't know their names, but they were surely professional religious artists from somewhere further to the south in New Spain, up here on a commission that might have taken them a number of years. We do know that no expense was spared on the materials—gold and silver leaf, the most costly available pigments. No white clay and red ochre for this project! In fact this is—and was—the most elaborate and expensive mission building in the entire region. You have to go to San Antonio, Texas, or Santa Fe, New Mexico, to see equally elaborate baroque details, and even then what you find are details, not an entire church.

A late-eighteenth-century document gives the reason for this: the church was deliberately built as a statement of the wonderful things that could happen in villages that invited missionaries to enter and stay. It was to be a "beacon of faith" to the as-yet-unconverted natives to the north and east. As things turned out, it was actually the semi-final gasp of a system of mission expansion that would soon run out of money and energy in a colony—New Spain—that in a few decades would be replaced by the independent nation of Mexico. But what a gasp!

This notion of a final burst of energy gets reinforced when one realizes that San Xavier is in fact an unfinished church. Not only was the eastern bell tower never finished, but a lot of brickwork inside the towers was left raw and unplastered.

Now it's easy to hear wonderful stories explaining this fact. One of the workers fell off the east tower, some say, and therefore the tower never got finished. Or the Spanish crown would levy taxes only on finished buildings … and so the tower was never completed. Or the east tower originally had a dome, but it was blown off by a cyclone and never replaced. Great stories, all of them, but there's not a shred of evidence that they are based on fact. The stark truth seems to be that the builders ran out of money. (I used to say in talks that the builders simply ran out of steam … until one member of the audience pointed out that steam was not used for construction in the late eighteenth century! Oh, well.) Finally, no matter what you read in the popular media Father Kino did not—repeat NOT—build any church at the site.

There are other stories as well, that take us into the realm of oral tradition and folklore. I was once told that the original dome of San Xavier was covered with a thin layer of gold, which had been mined locally by the missionaries. However, in the story this was stripped off by a later group of Spaniards. We'll get to the subject of hidden mission treasures later on in this book. Another belief attached to the church is that the angels on either side of the sanctuary were modeled after the beautiful twin daughters of one of the artists. The statues are indeed beautiful, especially since they were cleaned and repaired, but there is no documentary evidence for or against this story.

What is going on with all these stories seems simple: they are answers to perfectly natural questions concerning the church, worked out by people who did not have access to documents, but who had to rely upon logic, common sense, and imagination. Such questions include: "Why is the east tower unfinished?" "What were the missionaries really doing?" "Who served as models for the art?" And, last but not least, "What are that cat and mouse doing on the church façade?"

The cat and the mouse occupy the uppermost tier of relief sculpture on the church façade, crouched in full relief on the tops of the spiral motifs or volutes on either side of the façade. There they have sat since the church was built, glaring at each other. The explanation I hear most often is that "when the cat catches the mouse, it will be the end of the world." But that's an interpretation, rather than an explanation, of their presence. I suspect that when the world's Last Day does arrive, we will have other means to determine that fact than by watching the façade of San Xavier. I have also been told a long story about how these two natural enemies symbolize by their presence an ending of some sort of hostilities … but hostility by whom towards whom? The teller did not remember. The explanation I am most comfortable with is that all sorts of images can appear on baroque churches, and that doubtless the creators had a good idea of why the critters are there. But the answers are lost in time.

What is most emphatically not lost in time is the church itself. I'm not going to describe it here. I urge you to go out and see it, and read Bernard Fontana's booklet on its history or *A Gift of Angels,* his definitive study of the Mission's art. And when you visit (and this building deserves more than one trip), look at your fellow visitors. You'll soon discover that this wonderful building is actually several places in one, visited by a cross-section of people for a wide range of purposes.

First and foremost, it is a functioning Catholic church, administered by members of the Order of Friars Minor, or Franciscans. It still serves the native village for which it was built over 200 years ago. It is a pilgrimage destination: any weekend, people may be seen walking out from Tucson to pay respects to the reclining statue of Saint Francis Xavier in the west transept. It is also an important destination for people who are interested in Spanish Colonial religious art, having the largest collection of that art still *in situ* anywhere in the United States. It is a tourist destination as well—tour buses may often be found in the parking lot. It has an excellent small museum to interpret the building and its history to the general public. Some people even drive out just to buy Indian popovers or chile burritos at one or another of the booths in the plaza. And these are just a few of the roles this remarkable building plays in the world.

So there you have San Xavier Mission—the White Dove of the Desert. As I said, it's well worth a visit, and well worth reading about, for I haven't begun to tell you half of what there is to say about it.

THE YAQUIS AND YAQUI EASTER

Tucson is home to several communities of Yaqui Indians, a group whose traditional homeland lies some three hundred miles south of the border, along the Río Yaqui in Sonora. Although there has been a Yaqui presence in what is now Arizona for hundreds of years, the ancestors of many Arizona Yaquis moved north from Sonora in the late nineteenth and early twentieth centuries, escaping what amounted to a deliberate program of genocide on the part of the Mexican government. In Sonora, Yaquis were occupying lands on either bank of a year-round river that could be farmed intensively using the modern damming and irrigation techniques of the day. The Yaquis have always considered their lands sacred, to be defended with all their strength. Over the years this defense was carried out with great determination and courage. In the eyes of the Mexican government, the Yaquis were standing in the way of scientific progress, and would continue to do so while any of them were left. Therefore it was decided that the Yaquis had to go. Many were killed in battles with the Mexican army. Others were rounded up and sent as slave labor to the henequen plantations in far-off Yucatan. Others fled, singly and in groups, for the United States border. By the early twentieth century, small communities of Yaquis were scattered through southern Arizona, along the railroad and in mining camps—two kinds of labor they were familiar with.

As they became confident that they would not be persecuted in their new home for being Yaquis, they began to revive the ceremonies of their traditional Yaqui Catholicism. Jesuit missionaries had first been invited into Yaqui country in 1619, staying there till the Jesuits were expelled from New Spain in 1767. During this time the Yaquis had evolved a distinctly Yaqui form of Christianity, blending native and imported beliefs and practices in a truly unique way. It is this ceremonial system that put down new roots in Arizona, and this system that persists to this day in Yaqui communities on both sides of the international border. There are six of these communities in Arizona: four in the Tucson area, one in Marana, and one in Guadalupe, just west of Tempe. Each community centers around a Yaqui Catholic church.

The major ceremony of the Yaqui ritual year, the Lenten-Easter drama, takes place in and around each church except that of Marana. Marana Yaquis participate at one or another of the Tucson churches. The Yaqui Easter ceremony is actually a Passion play, which involves much of the community and lasts for the entire forty days of Lent. Drama was used by early missionaries in

Mexico and elsewhere as a teaching device, and it was so successful that almost 400 years later the Easter drama is presented in Yaqui communities all over Sonora and Arizona. I say "drama," but what happens is very unlike a play in the tradition to which we are accustomed.

This is the rough outline: Every Friday of Lent, a procession of men and women, led by a *maehto* or lay prayer leader, leaves the church and goes around the Stations of the Cross, which are white wooden crosses set up around the plaza in front of the church. They carry holy statues, and pray and sing at each station. From the first procession on, they are joined by some rather unusual-looking individuals: men with rattles at their waists and ankles, wearing tall masks that enclose their heads, and carrying painted wooden swords and daggers. These are the *chapayekas,* or sharp-nosed ones. They are soldiers, looking for a man they have heard about named Jesus Christ. When they find him, they intend to kill him. They do not speak, but communicate by clacking their weapons and shaking their waist rattles. They are clowns in a sense, but very menacing and scary clowns. They are part of a larger ritual group called the *fariseos* or Pharisees—a military-style organization that also includes unmasked individuals.

Each Friday the procession follows the Way of the Cross, and each Friday they are joined by increasing numbers of chapayekas and fariseos. The chapayekas keep getting bolder, mocking the church people, but shuddering when they hear holy names like "Dios" and "Jesucristo." These processions keep growing in size and intensity until the Saturday before Palm Sunday.

The eve of Palm Sunday is considered to be outside of Lent, and so a full-fledged fiesta takes place. This involves two important groups of ritual performers who have not appeared before. The *matachines* are men and boys who have dedicated themselves to the Virgin of Guadalupe, and do ritual dances in her honor. Clad in crowns and ribbons and carrying rattles and brightly feathered trident wands, they perform a kind of contradance (reminiscent of such European-derived dances as the "Virginia Reel") to the music of violins and guitars. Their performances are considered sacred, and the ground over which they have danced is Holy Ground till the end of time. Yaqui churches have wide doorways and dirt floors, so the matachines can dance right up to the altar when that is called for. One of the loveliest of the matachín dances is the winding and unwinding of the maypole. Like all their dances, it has its own special tunes, or *sonim*, which are an important part of the Yaqui artistic heritage.

The other group of ritual performers consists of the *pascolas* and the deer dancer and their musicians. Pascolas (the name means "Old Men of the Fiesta") are the necessary ritual hosts of any fiesta. If no pascolas are present, the occasion is not a fiesta. Wearing distinctive masks and costumes, they open and close the ceremony, dance, pass out cigarettes, and serve as clowns. They keep the people concentrated on the fact that a special occasion is going on. When the pascola, clad in breechcloth and leg-and-belt rattles, and with his small wooden mask on the back or side of his head, dances to the music of the violin and harp, he beats out the complicated time of the music with his feet. This is accentuated by the leg rattles, which are strings of dried moth cocoons, partially filled with seeds.

When he dances to the flute and drum (played by a single man), the pascola pulls his mask over his face and takes out his hand rattle, and his dance changes. Now his footwork is much simpler, and his head and upper body move back and forth in a peering motion, which allows full play to the horse or goat-hair beard of the mask. At this point he can be joined by the deer dancer.

If the matachines show strong European roots, and the pascolas appear to be a mix of the native and the imported, the deer dancer comes from a much older layer of Yaqui culture. His musical accompaniment consists of three of four singers who sing in an archaic form of Yaqui about the enchanted deer dancing in the "flowery world." Their instruments are also very old—rasping sticks on hollow gourd resonators and a drum consisting of a waxed gourd floating in a tub of water and beaten with a stick wrapped in corn husks. The pascolas interact with the deer, who remains aloof, occupying a world of his own. At some fiestas, the pascolas turn into hunters or coyotes and "kill" the deer.

These activities, alternating with the reciting of prayers and singing of hymns before a special fiesta altar, continue from dusk 'til shortly after dawn. The fariseos and chapayekas are also in evidence, marching with the processions and camped by a cross in front of the fiesta altar. Shortly after dawn the

Palm Sunday fiesta is over, and the tired participants look forward to Holy Week and the end of their ritual obligations.

Things slow down a bit until Holy Thursday. Then the intensity picks up. In the late afternoon, following several processions, Jesus is discovered by the chapayekas in the "Garden of Gethsemane" (a small thicket of desert willow branches) and taken round the Way of the Cross by triumphant chapayekas.

On Friday, the chapayekas pull up the crosses that stand in front of houses all over the village, and later on, Jesus is crucified, once more during a Way of the Cross procession. Each chapayeka taps a cross with the end of his sword. Finally, late at night, the chapayekas celebrate their victory. Jesus is placed in a decorated bier, and his captors and killers pretend to drink and dance. However, one by one they notice that the bier is empty, and one by one they wander off into the night.

They are back on Saturday morning, however, in full force—chapayekas, fariseos, and their allies. While the church party and the fiesta dancers and musicians file into the church, the Forces of Evil parade an effigy of their leader, Judas, around the plaza. They believe they have won. Judas is dressed as a chapayeka, stuffed with straw (and firecrackers), and tied to a pole at the far end of the plaza, from which vantage point he can watch their final victory. Finally all is ready, and chapayekas, fariseos, and their allies march from their camping place for the last time. They are tired now, not having slept for several days and having undergone other privations. They form up in two lines in front of the church, and, to the rhythmic clack of their wooden weapons, start to march towards that building—the last place in the village that they do not control. At a signal, they run towards the church, the bells ring, and the church party beats them off ... with confetti and green leaves. These represent flowers, which in Yaqui thought are God's blessings. Three times they charge, and three times they are beaten back. After the third charge they pile their masks and weapons next to Judas and rush into church to rededicate themselves to God and cleanse themselves from the vestiges of the role they have just played. Judas is set afire, and the firecrackers explode. After an interval, a procession carries the saints from the church to the fiesta altar, and the fiesta continues till after dawn on Easter Sunday, complete with matachines, deer dancer, pascolas, and the singing of hymns. The fariseos keep order, chop the wood for the fires, and do all the needed chores.

On Easter Sunday everyone who participated forms a circle in the plaza, and the head maehto gives a sermon of thanks, enumerating all of the roles played in the forty-day ceremony, from cooks to pascolas and musicians, to chapayekas. All are necessary parts of the enterprise, and all are thanked. Then, at long last, everyone can go home and catch a little sleep.

It is important to note that what I have presented is a highly condensed sketch of the complex and deeply meaningful events of the Yaqui Easter ceremony as it is presented in Tucson. I urge all interested readers to get a copy of Muriel Thayer Painter's forty-page booklet *A Yaqui Easter*, which gives a thoughtful and thorough explanation of the action. Although the ceremonies at the various Yaqui communities differ from each other in minor details, the outline as presented holds true for all.

Yaqui Easter is indeed a dramatic presentation, but it differs in several ways from the dramas we are accustomed to. In the first place, there are no individual actors who speak lines. Action and conflict are represented by the marching and counter-marching of members of ceremonial organizations, who have taken vows to participate. Another difference is a bit harder to express. When one goes to see *Hamlet*, for instance, one knows what will happen—how things will turn out. I get the strong impression that for at least some Yaquis the outcome of the drama is by no means assured. There is always the possibility that the wrong side might win. In each village where the drama takes place, something very important is being laid on the line. In every village, the Yaquis are "playing for keeps," ensuring that good will triumph over evil, at least for another year.

Fortunately for us all, Yaqui people are traditionally very open and welcoming about their Easter observances. Spectators have always been welcomed in Arizona's Yaqui communities. There are, however, certain rules that one must follow. First and foremost of these rules is that no cameras, recorders, sketch pads, or notebooks are allowed. Period. The only data retrieval systems we are allowed to use are those which were issued to us at birth. No alcohol, of course ... this is a religious ceremony. It is wise not to walk between a cross and the altar it stands in front of, and one should dress respectfully. And that's about it. In exchange you get to participate in one of the great occasions of beauty that occur in our region. I say "participate" because in Yaqui eyes, you are participating by your very presence. Through your attitude—whether or not you come to the ceremonies "with good heart"—you can add or detract from the effectiveness of the occasion. A great responsibility, but a great privilege as well.

For more detailed information on the Yaquis, you may turn to Muriel Thayer Painter's *With Good Heart: Yaqui Beliefs and Ceremonies in Pascua Village* and *The Yaquis: A Cultural History,* by Edward H. Spicer.

WATERLORE

I've heard it said that Southern Arizonans tend not to be strong church goers, for the following reason: for six months out of the year the weather is so perfect that nobody worries about going to heaven, and if you can survive a Sonoran Desert summer, the flames of hell hold no terrors. As I write this in early February, we are well into the heavenly phase of the cycle. Last week the daytime temperature was in the high seventies. Then the temperature dropped to freezing for a couple of nights, and we had about half an inch of gentle rain—what some people call "farmer's rain," the kind that soaks into the ground. In local Spanish these winter rains are called *equipatas,* a loan word from the Yaqui language meaning "gentle winter rains." A good word to try at a cocktail party: "Well, we should have some good equipatas this year." Nobody will know what you're talking about, but they will be impressed.

But winter inevitably fades into spring, and spring into summer. (Yes, Virginia, there really are four seasons here!) Even the hardened desert rats will admit that summer can get downright noticeable, especially in June, when the temperatures soar into three figures and the rains are perhaps a month off. In recent years, people have taken to calling those rains "the monsoon season."

When I was young, monsoons happened in the Indian Ocean, and our summer rains were called "the rainy season" or, in Spanish, *las aguas*—"the waters." I've always suspected that the word "monsoon" was introduced by outsiders eager to make our region more impressive by pretending it's someplace else. Be that as it may, the rains traditionally can start on June 24, Saint John the Baptist's Day, or *el Día de San Juan*. Saint John, who baptized Jesus in the River Jordan, is celebrated in all sorts of watery ways. Children and young adults hold water fights on his day. In years past, people would have picnics by any available body of water, and go bathing. Water, because it was used for such a sacred purpose, is believed by many to have special powers on that day, and cures for eye problems were traditionally sought by washing the eyes in a stream. And now the rains can legitimately begin.

There's a bit of weather prophesying here, too. If the rains do begin on the Día de San Juan, the belief goes, that's a sign that there will be really good summer rains. But if they begin before June 24, San Juan is trying to warn us of some disaster like famine or pestilence. However, for that to hold true it has to rain all over the valley. A few drops in one place don't count.

This business of it raining all over the valley brings us to another characteristic of our summer rains: they are extremely localized. It is not unusual to have a half-inch or more of rain in one spot, and nothing at all a mile away. In fact, I heard of a man who left his double-barreled shotgun leaning against a fence post near his house. When he came back next morning to retrieve it, he found the left barrel full of water and the right one full of cobwebs.

And when it does rain, it really rains! Water sheets down to the ground, dry streets and washes become flowing rivers in minutes, and unwary drivers can get trapped in their cars by the rushing waters of a flash flood. These floods can appear like magic, in the form of a wall of water rushing down from mountains so distant that one doesn't think about them. Those true summer "toad-strangling gully washers" are to be treated with the greatest respect. It really is possible to drown in the middle of Tucson.

But the rain brings life as well as, and more consistently than, death. After the rains start, the desert perks up, summer crops grow, and the wild, edible greens called *quelites* and *verdolagas* spring out of the soil. People, too, seem to get happier once it starts to rain. In this part of the world, rain is a blessing rather than an inconvenience. Mexicano musicians, if they are to be paid for a job, will say *"va a llover"*—"it's going to rain." If the pay seems truly generous, the phrase is *"se van a caer rayos"*—"thunderbolts are going to fall."

Of course all this can have its silly side as well. One July day back in 1937, a young newspaperman at the *Arizona Daily Star* named Howard O. Welty found himself bored with the lack of interesting local news. So he decided to make some up, and wrote a story about young Elmira Doakes, daughter of Joseph Doakes of Tucson, who was the first person to swim across the pond that forms in the Stone Avenue Underpass after a heavy rain. The story caught folks' fancy, and the body of water became known as "Lake Elmira." A few years later, it was reported that certain city interests were applying for a grant to chlorinate Lake Elmira and build a marina on its south shore. In the 1980s, a couple of public-spirited Tucsonans fabricated a phony historical marker, in English and Spanish. One dark night, they affixed it to the south side of the railroad bridge on Stone Avenue, where it stood for many years.

When I first arrived in Tucson, I was told the following joke: A Tucson lady was visiting an old school chum who lived by the banks of the Hudson River. After she had stayed for a few days, her hostess couldn't contain herself. "How do you like our beautiful Hudson River?" she asked. "I don't know," replied the lady from Arizona. "I haven't had a chance to get a look at it. It's been full of water all the time!"

The special nature of what we call "rivers" in this country—long, skinny stretches of sand and rocks over which water flows after a rain—has led to one of southern Arizona's most famous tall tales: the Southern Arizona Sand Trout. You see, while the desert was drying out after the last Ice Age, the trout that lived in the local streams slowly evolved in order to survive in their changing environment. Their gills changed into lungs, and their eyes grew on stalks. These modifications allowed them to "swim" along just under the surface of the sand, looking out into the air. Thus they could catch insects, small lizards, and other prey.

Very shy, and able to see long distances, they became known as Arizona's prime game fish. It was hard to catch them, as the angler must remain totally concealed during the process. This was not impossible in the case of handy large boulders in the stream bed, but if the banks of the wash were lined, as they so often are, with mesquite thickets, one could make just one cast in the morning, and then spend the rest of the day untangling one's line. Finally some genius hit upon the idea of using horned toads ("horny toads" in common speech) as bait. One could dispense with hooks and simply tie the line around the critters' bellies, behind their front legs. When the fish struck, a quick jerk would set the lizard's spikes in the fish's gullet. If the fisherman hauled the trout to shore briskly, the friction of the desert sands would have it skinned and cooked by the time it was landed.

One must remember, however, always to release the bait. Horny toads are a protected species, but there is no law on the books that says you can't take them for little walks in the desert.

For the definitive popular study on horned toads, more properly called "horned lizards," see Wade C. Sherbrooke's *Introduction to Horned Lizards of North America.* An equivalent scientific discussion of the sand trout has yet to be written.

Those wishing a more traditional way to prepare sand trout for the table could do worse than try the following traditional recipe: Mix a marinade consisting of five parts tequila, three parts red chile, and one part lime juice. Marinate the sand trout overnight. At the end of that time, feed the fish to the dogs and drink the marinade.

This sort of story seems to have been created for a specific kind of entertainment: the joy of fooling outsiders. The trick, of course, is to preserve a perfectly straight face while trolling for your sucker. Several years ago, our breakfast group was joined by a visitor from Minnesota. Several of the group are avid fishermen, and we discovered that the Minnesotan was one also. Very slowly the gang started to discuss sand trout. The visiting fisherman had never heard of such critters, and listened excitedly. It was about ten minutes into the conversation when he finally realized that his leg was being pulled. He never joined us again.

One more piece of sand trout information: As you drive along Tanque Verde Road in northeast Tucson, look to either side as you cross the Rose Hill Wash near Trail Dust Town. There you will see shining metal sculptures of leaping fish, executed by local artist Chris Tanz. She told me that the piece was inspired by our sand trout.

Not all the lore connected with rivers and bodies of water in this region, however, is light-hearted. For riverbeds and irrigation ditches are also known as the haunt of La Llorona, the Weeping Woman. She is known all over Mexico, and there are several stories about her. One relates how she drowned her children many years ago, in order to follow a young man she was in love with, and was doomed to haunt rivers for all eternity, looking for her lost babies. A purely local story tells how she was a Tucson mother who told her little boy not to play in the dry washes in the summer. He did, of course, and was carried off in a flood. She went mad with grief and is still hunting for him ... or any other child she can find. Her story is told to children by parents as a way of keeping them safely home, especially at night. Irrigation ditches and river bottoms can be dangerous places for a number of reasons, not all of which involve scary ladies clad in white. The point is that the stories are terrifying enough to be believed. I have Mexicano friends who have seen her, dressed in white, screaming and crying along the Santa Cruz and others of our rivers. And she is not confined just to Tucson or southern Arizona. Wherever Mexicanos have settled, they have taken La Llorona with them. She is all over Mexico, of course ... but she has also been seen on the Chicago waterfront, and along the Mississippi near Minneapolis. She is always grief-stricken, always crazy, always seeking children.

Folklore is always dynamic, if it is to remain a living part of culture, and in the last thirty years La Llorona's name has become attached to the more contemporary legend of the girl who died in the girls' restroom in elementary school. Her story is known to young girls all over the country. In other places she is known as Mary Jane or Bloody Mary or Mary Whales. On the southwest side of Tucson, her name is La Llorona. If you stand in the girls' restroom with the lights out and repeat some such formula as "La Llorona, you murdered your babies," twenty times, you can see her coming at you out of the mirror. Only almost nobody has the courage to make the test.

There is a lot of literature on La Llorona. Two good articles on her local manifestations were written by Betty Leddy in 1948 and 1950, and published in the journal *Western Folklore*. They are listed in the bibliography.

It's a long way from the winter rains in Tucson to a scary story in the girls' restroom. The unifying factor, of course, seems to be water. That is the most precious commodity we have, and potentially a deadly one as well.

CHAPTER TWO

The Trek Continues, with Digressions and a Calendar

I WARNED YOU THAT OUR TRAVELS ON THIS TREASURE HUNT through our region's traditions would involve side trips and digressions. Here's one.

HORSE RACES, SONGS, AND MUSIC

If you go to any fiesta in Sonora, one activity you are likely to find is horse racing. Match racing, to be more precise, in which two horses, often from different ranches or communities, run against each other. This elevates the sport to a sort of personal combat, always a favorite subject for Mexican poets. In Texas, they sing:

Que bonito ver dos hombres
Que se matan, pecho a pecho
Cada con pistola en mano
Defendiendo a su derecho.

How beautiful it is to see two men
Who kill each other, chest to chest
Each with a pistol in his hand,
Defending his rights.

These lines are from "Arnulfo Gonzales," a famous *corrido* or ballad dating back to revolutionary times. Corridos are still being composed and sung all over Mexico and the Pimería and provide an often pithy commentary on their times. (Nowadays the heroes are often *narcotraficantes*—drug smugglers—who may commission poets to write corridos about them to increase their prestige.) However, many of the older corridos are still sung and requested and loved. Favorite corrido topics include incidents of the Revolution, disasters, horrible crimes, praise of beloved hometowns, brave deeds of brave men … and horse races, in which two horses take the place of human heroes.

These latter comprise a favorite corrido topic in Sonora and Arizona. By horse races, I'm referring to match races. Crowds gather, folks get very excited, and large sums of money are often bet. I personally have heard horse race corridos dating back to the 1890s, and the genre is still very much alive. The most famous of these horse race corridos is "El Moro de Cumpas" ("The Grey Horse from Cumpas"), about a race that took place in the streets of Agua Prieta, Sonora, on March 17, 1957, between Relámpago (Lightning), a locally owned chestnut, and "El Moro," from the village of Cumpas, on the Río Moctezuma.

The song, composed by Leonardo Yáñez of Agua Prieta, starts like this:

El diecisiete de marzo	On March seventeenth
A la ciudad de Agua Prieta	To the city of Agua Prieta
Llegó gente de dondequiera,	People came from all over.
Vinieron a la carrera	They came for the race
De Relámpago y El Moro,	Between Relámpago and El Moro,
Dos caballos de primera.	Two first-class horses.

After describing the race and the excitement leading up to it, Yáñez apologizes in the last verse because Relámpago won and el Moro, the favorite, lost. This song is still requested in bars where itinerant musicians play for tips, and customers occasionally ask the musicians: "Play 'El Moro de Cumpas' until el Moro wins!" Only last year I heard the last verse changed around so that that was indeed the case. There is a monument in Agua Prieta at the finish line of the race, and a more-than-life-sized statue of el Moro stands on the turnoff from the highway to Cumpas, in Sonora. More about this race and its songs may be found in Chapter 7 of *A Shared Space*.

Now we move from heroic horses to heroic people. Cast your mind back to September 11, 2001, and the hijacking of four commercial jetliners by terrorists. Only three of those planes made it to their intended targets. The fourth, United Airlines Flight 93, crashed where it could do no harm after its passengers had tried to retake it. That, my friends, is bravery. Those folks knew that they were dead already, but summoned the presence of mind to act in order to save more lives. If you're looking for real heroes, you need look no farther.

There is an example of that sort of heroism just across the border, in the Sonoran mining town of Nacozari. On Thursday, November 7, 1907, an engine driver named Jesús García made ready for his afternoon run out to the mines at nearby Pilares. This was a routine trip, carrying tools and supplies. Among the latter was dynamite. As the train left the yard, sparks from a faulty smokestack lit a fire in a car loaded with explosives. García took in the situation, told his crew to jump, and made a desperate try to get the train out of the narrow valley in which the town lay and to a place where he could safely jump and let the deadly train go harmlessly off the track. He almost made it before the dynamite blew up. García and a few others were killed; one hates to think how many more would have died had the train not left town.

The mining town of Nacozari remains, but it has been renamed Nacozari de García in honor of the brave engineer. A civic celebration and tribute take place annually on or about November 7, and one may well hear the corrido honoring this famous deed at that time. It is called "Máquina 501" ("Engine Number 501") and starts as follows:

Máquina quinientos uno	Engine Five Hundred and One,
La que corrió por Sonora	The one that ran through Sonora,
Por eso los garroteros	That's why the brakeman
El que no suspira, llora.	Who doesn't sigh, cries.

When Jesús realizes what is happening, his fireman begs him to jump and save his life. Our hero replies, with words undoubtedly placed in his mouth by the corrido composer:

Jesús García le contesta	Jesús García answers him
"Yo pienso muy diferente.	"I think very differently.
Yo no quiero ser la causa	I don't wish to be the cause
De que muera tanta gente."	Of so many people dying."

And there you have it. That's heroism, no matter where or in what century it happens.

The story of Jesús García is told in detail and with wonderful old photographs by Don Dedera in his book *In Search of Jesús García*. The two corridos mentioned here, along with other corridos from our border region, may be found on the CD entitled *Heroes and Horses: Corridos of the Arizona-Sonora Borderlands.*

The kind of band that one might find singing this and other corridos in a bar is called a *conjunto norteño* or "northern style group." Its members would wear Western clothes and cowboy hats, and would play button accordion, a small stand-up bass, and a twelve-stringed bass guitar called a *bajo sexto*. Sometimes a saxophone and snare drum are added to the lineup. These groups specialize in polkas, corridos, romantic boleros, and *canciones rancheras,* which are the Mexican equivalent of our country western songs of the 50s and 60s.

Other Mexican musical groups you might find in restaurants and bars include guitar and vocal duets, and mariachis. These latter include trumpets, violins, and three sizes of guitar: the tiny, five-stringed *vihuela,* the regular guitar, and the huge *guitarrón,* which looks for all the world like a six-stringed bathtub. Mariachis wear the elaborate costume of the *charro,* or central Mexican cowboy. Mariachis can and may play anything, from "Rancho Grande" to "The Orange Blossom Special," but the core of the mariachi repertoire is the *son jaliciense,* the traditional folk dance music of the state of Jalisco, where the art form originated. Since its development in the 1930s, mariachi has become the visual and musical symbol of the artistic soul of Mexico.

Of course, even within the limits of Mexican music available in the Pimería, there are many other forms—the Oompah sound of the *banda* which is currently popular among younger dancers, *la música tropical*, complete with congas and maracas, and various forms of contemporary popular music. We live in a musical place.

According to some ways of thinking, it can get too musical, with too many opportunities to make the wrong decisions in the excitement of a dance. The story is told in Tucson and all over the border about a young girl who was told by her mother not to attend a public dance. She argued with her mother and went anyway. While at the dance she met a handsome young stranger from outside the neighborhood. He was really cute and a great dancer, and he only wanted to dance with this one girl. So they danced together a lot. Nobody could see that there was anything wrong about him except one poor girl who had come to the dance hall to sell flowers or matches or something. She wasn't involved in the excitement, so she could see more clearly than others ... and when she looked at the young man's feet, she started screaming, "*Pato de gallo! Pato de gallo!*" ("Rooster foot! Rooster foot!") It was the Devil. The couple just kept on dancing faster and faster until they both disappeared, and, as the old lady who first told me this story said grimly, "Perhaps they're still dancing ... somewhere!"

This story still lives in Mexican American families, but in a specialized way. When I ran it past the students in my folklore class, few of the Chicanos had heard it, but most of the Chicanas knew it well. It is told to girls as a cautionary tale—the ultimate proof that Mother knows best.

BARRIO STREET ART

For this stage of our journey, we need to go to Tucson's west and southwest sides, to the west of the Santa Cruz River and north of "A" Mountain, for instance, and the residential area centering on Sixth Avenue and stretching from Downtown to around Irvington Road. These areas include many of our named barrios, and abound in various sorts of art, all visible from the city streets. Let's look at front yards first.

The typical Mexican front yard in Tucson is separated from the street by some sort of fence—chain link, wrought iron, masonry, or a combination of the last two. Such fences may be strictly utilitarian or highly decorative. Their usual height is between three and four feet. There is a strong possibility that this custom is what happens when an old cultural tradition of building dwellings out to the sidewalk or the street, as they are in Mexico and some of the oldest parts of town, collides with urban zoning regulations that require a setback from the street. The result is an extension of private space out to the edge of the property, rather than the somewhat ambiguous public/private space created by the mainstream front lawn or garden.

This private space is traditionally the realm of the woman of the house. Rather than the lawn commonly found in other parts of town, it is usually a patch of bare dirt, often kept carefully raked. These front yards are often quite formally laid out, with trees and shrubs bordered with rings of small rocks. What smaller plants there are may be decorative or useful as herbs, and are usually set in containers rather than in the bare earth. These containers are often the recycled mementos of family or close friends, serving to remind the woman of the house of the social network in which she lives.

If the yard contains a shrine, it, too, is supervised by the woman of the house. Shrines are often erected in front yards in repayment of some favor a particular saint is believed to have granted the family—little reminders of disaster averted. The shrines are usually lit up in some way, and contain the statue of the saint involved, along, perhaps, with other saints especially loved by the family. When a house with a shrine is sold to new owners who do not wish to use it, they will frequently let it stand empty rather than tear it down.

Walls, whether they belong to buildings or are used to enclose spaces, present wonderful possibilities for public art. These are responded to on a number of levels. Graffiti represent one very informal, unauthorized response. They can have the social function of marking off a neighborhood or "turf"—an activity that happens as well among other mammals—think of dogs and fire hydrants.

They can also provide an opportunity to satisfy both the creative urge and a desire for relative danger—a not uncommon pair of impulses among the young of Homo sapiens. They are illegal, so it's a bit risky to put them up. The simpler, self-identifying graffiti are called "tags"; the more elaborate are called "pieces." Although these graffiti are regarded as art by their creators and have a small following of fans, many people regard them as acts of vandalism. Occasional attempts on the part of local authorities to encourage tagging and pieces in specific areas have been met by strong public disapproval.

On a more formal and acceptable level are the cultural murals that exist all over the south and west sides of town. These started showing up on public and commercial buildings in the late 1960s, and are the work of a relatively small cadre of professional and semi-professional artists. Most of these murals—but not all—celebrate Mexican American and Chicano culture, employing images of Aztecs, the Virgin of Guadalupe, low-rider cars, and other cultural symbols for the purpose. An artist may get a grant for a mural in a school or on a public building, enlist neighborhood youth or a class as helpers, design the mural, and then execute it. In 1993 the Tucson Pima Arts Council published *Murals: Guide to Murals in Tucson.* By now, of course, it is both out of date and out of print, but local libraries should have copies. It lists the title (if any), artist, location, and date of 135 local murals.

The Virgin of Guadalupe deserves special mention here. She is the Virgin Mary as she is believed to have appeared to an Aztec Indian named Juan Diego (San Juan Diego since his elevation to sainthood in 2002 by Pope John Paul II) just outside of Mexico City. The year was 1531, and Mexico had only recently been incorporated into the Spanish Empire, when a beautiful woman appeared to Juan Diego, identifying herself as the Mother of God, and asking that a church be built in her honor on that spot. After Juan Diego had little success in convincing the bishop in Mexico City that the apparition was a true one, the Virgin instructed him to pick the roses that were growing on the hill, and carry them as a sign to the bishop wrapped in his cloak or *tilma*. Juan Diego did as he was told, only to discover that the tilma itself had been mysteriously imprinted with an image of the Virgin. It is this tilma that is still on display in the basilica of the Virgin of Guadalupe in Mexico City today, and this image that has been reproduced millions of times, in every conceivable medium. Guadalupe appears on walls, in murals, engraved in precious metals, on jewelry, on clothing, on low-rider cars, and virtually everywhere else in the Mexican and Mexican American worlds. She is ubiquitous, "the mother of us all," as one friend put it. She brings together diverse peoples, stands up for the underdogs, and, with her dark skin, proudly proclaims a mixed ancestry of Spanish and Indian.

One of the places Our Lady of Guadalupe shows up is on the hoods, trunks, and windows of low-rider cars. Developed in post-war California, low riders, those elaborately customized automobiles that one Chicano poet has called "butterflies with transmissions," have spread all over the country, wherever there are sizeable Chicano populations. You can start with almost any car, lower it, install hydraulic lifters on all four wheels, customize the body to whatever extent you wish, give it an elaborate, multi-coat paint job, perhaps add a mural or two, and make the interior as luxurious as possible. You can give it a name: "Bad Enuff," "Wild Thing," or perhaps "Garfield" (after the comic-strip cat). If you intend to enter it in a low-rider show, you will make up a beautiful sign listing all the individuals and shops that have had a hand in the creation process. At the end of all this, you will have created a complex statement of elegance over efficiency, saying in effect that the speed with which you travel is nowhere near as important as the style with which you arrive. This in itself is a negation of mainstream American values, and a strong statement of cultural identity.

There are also low-rider bikes. They can be as complex, luxurious, and basically impractical as the cars. But remember that here we are not talking practicality but style.

More discussion—and illustrations—of Mexican American street art may be found in my book, *Hecho a Mano: The Traditional Arts of Tucson's Mexican American Community.*

Now let's move out of the city and travel along suburban and rural roads in southern Arizona. Another kind of street art calls attention to itself—art that is found on boundaries. This includes mailbox supports and custom-made gates.

Within a couple of miles of where I live, I have found and photographed a mailbox support made out of a motorcycle, another that includes a real saddle, and a saguaro crafted from horseshoes. In the same short stretch of road there is also a wide gate bearing the cutout silhouette of San Xavier Mission. And all four of these occur within half a mile of each other!

Ethnicity takes a back seat here. Most of these seem rather to be public statements of where we are and what we find of interest. In a similar vein one can often find old bits of agricultural equipment recycled into mailbox supports. It all adds up to make any drive around the outskirts of town an adventure. A short discussion of this "boundary art" appears in yet another of my books, *Southern Arizona Folk Arts,* but the scene is so dynamic and changing that it is really up to you to find your own masterpieces.

A ROUND OF HOLIDAYS

Tucson is a wonderful place in which to enjoy a round of Mexican cultural and religious holidays. Let's tackle the cultural ones first.

By far the most important of these is *El Dieciseis de Septiembre,* September 16, or Mexican Independence Day. This is the date in 1811 on which Father Miguel Hidalgo rang the church bell in the village of Guadalupe (now Guadalupe Hidalgo), and cried out *"¡Viva México!"* and *"¡Viva la Virgen de Guadalupe!"* and other excited slogans from the church balcony, starting the ten-year War of Liberation from Spain. This same cry is echoed each year from every seat of national, state, or local government throughout Mexico. Not, however, in Arizona. Here the day is indeed celebrated by many Mexican Americans, but as an affirmation of cultural pride and historical identity, rather than as a political occasion.

The other great secular Mexican holiday, actually more popular in the United States than in many parts of Mexico, is May 5, El Cinco de Mayo. This commemorates the Battle of Puebla in 1862, where Mexican troops under General Ignacio Zaragoza defeated a French army outside the city of Puebla. Never mind that the French returned and occupied all of Mexico, putting Maximilian of Austria on the throne as Emperor. This ill-fated regime lasted only till 1867, when the royalist troops were defeated and the Emperor executed. The incident, including the departure into exile of the Empress Carlota, is still remembered in Tucson in the children's rhyme:

Adiós Mamá Carlota,	Goodbye Mama Carlota
Narices de pelota.	Nostrils like a ball.
Adiós Papá Agustín,	Goodbye Papa Agustín,
Narices de violín.	Nostrils like a violin.

"Papá Agustín" refers to Agustín Iturbide, who made himself Emperor of Mexico directly after Independence from Spain. Thus Mexico's two experiments with royalty are preserved in a children's song whose twin messages are "You look weird," and "Goodbye."

Every year in February, Tucson holds its annual rodeo—"La Fiesta de los Vaqueros." This a week-long celebration of our regional cattle-raising roots, complete with an old-time fiddle contest, "the country's longest non-motorized parade," license to wear "western clothing" to work, and several days of professional rodeo. Rodeo, by the way, is a series of contests drawing upon skills that were important for cowboy work in the old, open-range days (such as riding bucking horses and roping calves) along with other, more spectacular sports such as bull riding and steer wrestling.

The Presidio de Tucson was founded in August, and the whole month has recently been set aside for the celebration of Tucson's birthday. Flags are raised, historically costumed soldiers march, and a whole kaleidoscope of activities takes place. Finally, the second weekend in October is the time for Tucson Meet Yourself, a folklife festival (already mentioned in these pages) that has been going since 1974 in downtown El Presidio Park.

Of course these aren't the only holidays celebrated by Tucsonans—and some at least have a special flavor to them. I know of one Chinese-Mexican family who, on Thanksgiving, always prepare a turkey as though it were a Peking Duck—a custom started by an excellent cook a generation ago. And several

Mexican families make it a point to eat "Americano" food on the Fourth of July—hot dogs with all the fixings and potato salad. The Glorious Fourth often features fireworks on "A" Mountain (funded in 2009 in part by the Pascua Yaqui Tribe), and some neighborhoods have their own homegrown Fourth of July parades. In recent years, the African American community near "A" Mountain has been celebrating "Juneteenth" on or about June 19, in commemoration of the day on which news of emancipation arrived in Texas.

Equally interesting are the religious holidays and celebrations. Perhaps it is best to begin with Christmas, or rather with the day of the Virgin of Guadalupe, December 12. This is celebrated with a special Mass at the Cathedral, with pageants or short plays in many west side Catholic churches, and with the erection of special altars and decorations inside and outside the house in many west side homes. As the apparition is believed to involve roses growing on a cactus-covered hill, both roses and cacti may feature in the temporary Guadalupe altars. One town in Sonora, Querobabi, which is located about one and a half hours' drive from the border, celebrates the day in a particularly lovely fashion. There is an evening procession featuring floats bearing scenes of the Virgin appearing to Juan Diego, with live actors. The floats are constructed on one-ton flatbed trucks, one from each barrio of the town. Householders living along the procession route often erect their own outdoor Guadalupe altars, making for an evening of beauty in what is usually a small, dusty Sonoran town.

El Día de Guadalupe seems to be the signal in many Mexicano homes for Christmas preparations to begin. Many families erect a *nacimiento* or Nativity scene. This can be a simple set including the Holy Family, shepherds, and Wise Men, or it can be infinitely more elaborate, featuring scenes from the Old and New Testaments, Mexican villages and markets, and just about anything else one can imagine. Local newspapers will often give suggestions as to the location of special scenes. One notable nacimiento is set up every year at San Xavier Mission. It depicts the Nativity taking place among Tohono O'odham, under a ramada. The Baby Jesus lies in an old-fashioned hanging cradle, with a string leading to the front of the altar. Many people will come to the scene, say a short prayer, pull the string, and rock the Baby.

By far Tucson's most famous nacimiento is the one that was erected annually in the Tucson Museum of Art's La Casa Cordova by María Luisa Tena. In 2009 it became a permanent exhibit, saving Señora Tena the two months it took to rebuild it every fall. It occupies an entire room of La Casa Cordova, and includes, along with the expectable Holy Family, angels, shepherds, and wise men, scenes from the Bible, the apparition of the Virgin of Guadalupe, a Mexican ranch and market, and a Southwestern Indian pueblo. The message it gives to the viewer seems to be that the event it celebrates is not localized, but rather belongs to all times and places.

Holidays need special foods, and just as American Thanksgiving calls for turkey, so does Mexican Christmas demand tamales. Tamales date back to a time long before the Spanish conquest, and may be of many kinds. Christmas tamales in our region are made from shredded beef (or venison, if there have been lucky hunters in the family), cooked in a red chile sauce, surrounded by corn *masa* or dough, wrapped in cornhusks, and steamed. The preparation of the masa from finely ground corn that has been soaked in lye to release its enzymes, and then kneaded with water and shortening, is an arduous task, and most families go to a local tortilla factory to buy theirs ready-made. Then the assembly line work begins. It usually takes a whole family to put the tamales together, and they are put together in heroic quantities. Not only must all members of the extended family have all the tamales they can eat on Christmas Eve, but the delicacies are given away by the dozen. Nobody uses a written recipe—the senior woman directs the whole process—and it is always fun to taste other families' tamales (and realize that Mother's tamales are the best of all!). Many Anglo families have had their first taste of tamales when they moved to Tucson and their Mexican neighbors came over with a ziplock bag full of those Christmastime goodies. "Tamales," by the way, is the plural; "tamal" is the singular.

Christmas can involve two distinct kinds of dramatic performance: Las Posadas and the Pastorela. Both are handed down from the early days of Spanish Mexico, when the missionary priests used drama to teach the Indians under their charge the basic Christian narratives. Las Posadas is a dramatization of Joseph and Mary's search for lodging (the word means "the Inns" and is usually sponsored by Tucson's west side Catholic churches, although Carillo Elementary School has been doing a one-night Posada for over fifty years. The usual Posadas last nine nights, in which a procession walks residential streets, carrying statues of the Holy Couple and singing hymns in Spanish. They will stop at a prearranged house and request in song to be allowed to come in and rest.

One common song starts out this way:

¿Quién les da posada	Who will give shelter
A estos peregrinos	To these pilgrims
Quienes vienen cansados	Who arrive tired
De andar los caminos?	From traveling the roads?

Without opening the door, the folks in the house sing a song explaining that they don't take in strangers. At about the third house, however, once more by prearrangement, the doors are flung open and the "Holy Pilgrims" are welcomed in. All are fed cookies and a kind of hot chocolate drink called *champurrada,* the statues are placed on a special altar, and everything waits till the next night, when the scenes are repeated at different houses. Finally, on the ninth night the procession ends at the parish hall, where there is a party, and a star-shaped piñata is broken. This usually happens just before Christmas Eve. Then on Christmas Eve, people may attend midnight Mass and go home for a grand tamal feast. There—I've made myself hungry!

Champurrada, by the way, is made from toasted flour, Mexican chocolate, *piloncillo* (Mexican hard brown sugar), cinnamon, and cloves. It has a water base. Try it and work out your own proportions.

The Pastorela, or Shepherds' Play, is another Christmastime drama with roots in the sixteenth century. It portrays a group of shepherds journeying towards Bethlehem to see the newborn Child. They are hindered by the Devil and his minions, and different versions of the play can be filled with local allusions. "A Tucson Pastorela" has been presented annually since 1995 by Borderlands Theater. They rewrite the script each year, being sure to put in contemporary allusions. The devils, as they have in religious popular drama since the Middle Ages, supply the comedy. They can take the form of Hollywood or TV moguls, offering fame and fortune to the shepherds if they will only turn aside from their task; they may offer other sorts of temptations as well; and make threats too. The scene can often be set on the border, so the Devils may assume the role of Minutemen or other anti-immigrant zealots. Each obstacle threatens to halt or deflect the poor shepherds, but they are inevitably rescued by the Archangels Gabriel and Michael. At the end, the Three Kings arrive riding huge horse, camel, and elephant piñatas; the shepherds reach their goal; and the play ends in a burst of Christmas hope.

Moving away from Mexican culture, Christmas time is also the season for Tucson's residential neighborhood of Winterhaven to hold its annual Festival of Lights. Almost every house in that midtown area is decorated for Christmas, often very elaborately indeed, and the streets are filled with private cars and tour buses as Tucsonans and others enjoy the beauty of the season.

On Twelfth Night (January 6), known in Spanish as *el Día de Los Reyes* or Three Kings' Day, some families hold yet another celebration. At this time, a ring-shaped cake called *la rosca de los reyes,* containing one or more tiny images of the Baby Jesus, is cut and the pieces distributed. Whoever gets the Babies is responsible for putting on the last fiesta of the Christmas season on February 2, or *el Día de la Candelaria*, at which time the Baby is provided with a new set of clothes. The Day of the Kings is also the traditional day for the exchange of gifts in Mexican culture, even though more and more in Mexican households in the United States this takes place on Christmas Day.

Lent in the Catholic Church is a time of fasting and spiritual preparation, and there are many special, meatless dishes associated with these forty days before Easter. Among them is *capirotada,* a kind of bread pudding containing bread, cheese, dried fruits of several kinds, and nuts. I have already described Yaqui Easter; many local Mexicanos traditionally celebrate this joyous day by having a picnic, either out in the desert or in a local park.

Then on November 2 comes the Day of the Dead, or *el Día de los Muertos* (All Souls' Day in the Catholic church). The traditional local way of observing this day is to clean and redecorate the family graves, and, through memories and stories, bring the family dead back to mind, if not to life. Some cemeteries are filled with candles, especially those at San Xavier Mission and the village of Oquitoa in Sonora. Where it is allowed, floral tributes are placed on the newly cleaned graves.

The rich Día de los Muertos imagery of central and southern Mexico, with its candy skulls, its skeletons doing everyday things, and its social and political satire, has not made it across the border to any extent, outside of shops specializing in Mexican crafts ... with one significant exception: *pan de muerto* or Day of the Dead bread.

Many of Tucson's Mexican bakeries sell this special, rich bread in preparation for this day. Made with eggs in the dough and granulated sugar sprinkled on top, it takes the form of skulls, people, or round loaves with bones molded on them. There are several Mexican bakeries listed in Tucson's Yellow Pages; each one may sell a different shape of pan de muerto, depending on where in Mexico the master baker comes from.

In recent years, Tucson has staged a Day of the Dead parade as well, in which participants dress in fanciful costumes and honor their dead. This custom seems to be derived from a Chicano adaptation of the traditional Day of the Dead imagery of southern Mexico. It is a celebration of ancestors as well as an occasion to publicly honor the recently deceased, or present such life-and-death causes as illegal border crossings in the desert (which all too often end in the death of the crosser). It draws heavy participation from Tucson's arts communities, and has become an extremely popular and colorful event, with cultural, social, and political overtones. Although everyone who wishes to participates in the parade, most of the participants are Anglo Americans.

CRAFTS ACROSS CULTURES

Two wonderful craft forms that have taken root in Tucson deserve special mention here: piñatas and *cascarones*. Both are made out of colored tissue paper or *papel de china* (Chinese paper), so called because this craft came across the Pacific on the fabled Manila Galleons. Both are elaborately decorated objects whose function is to be broken at parties, adding more fun to the social occasion. Piñatas are large containers of papier-mâché, which are filled with candies and broken by blindfolded children, each of whom is given three tries at hitting the piñata with a stick. Piñatas can be in any shape—animal, vegetable, or human.

Cascarones are eggshells that have been emptied, refilled with confetti, often mounted on paper cones, and then decorated with colored paper, paint, feathers, and glitter. They, too, can come in many shapes.

Both art forms have passed over into mainstream American culture … but with a difference. Some Anglos use them in just the same ways that Mexicans do. But for other Anglos, they have become wall decorations—inexpensive bits of regional folk art that bring with them a sense of place, and signal to visitors that this household appreciates aspects of local culture.

And there you have a glimpse of Tucson's folklore and folklife. In Chapter Three, we will start moving south across the border, and explore the various legacies of Father Kino and his fellow missionaries.

Pilgrimage Paths

IT ALL STARTED WITH ONE MAN—an Italian Jesuit named Eusebio Francisco Kino. Born in 1645 in Segno, in what was then part of Austria and what is now northern Italy, he joined the Jesuit Order (the Society of Jesus) after recovering from a life-threatening illness. He took as his personal patron saint Francis Xavier, the Jesuit patron of missionaries, and had hopes of following him to China and the Far East. He was assigned, however, to the Jesuit missions in New Spain and started working in Baja California. That effort had to be temporarily abandoned, as the local resources just couldn't support a mission establishment. He was reassigned to northwest Sonora, to the mission community of Cucurpe ("Where the Dove Calls"), on the Río San Miguel. It was from Cucurpe that, on March 14, 1687, he rode westward into history.

Cucurpe was a recently established mission to the Ópata Indians. Just to the west was the beginning of a new tribal territory—that of the people who called themselves "O'odham" ("The People") and whom the Spaniards called Pimas. It was in this Pimería Alta or "Upper Pima Country," that Father Kino spent the rest of his life.

That date, March 14, 1687, marked an important beginning and ending for the Pimería Alta. Nothing was ever the same after Father Kino's arrival. He brought with him a new religion—Catholic Christianity. He brought wheat and cattle—and to this day our local traditional diet leans heavily on these two foodstuffs. Before his arrival, the O'odham were their own people, living off their resources, both physical and spiritual, and fighting with their neighbors when that was necessary. After Kino, like it or not, and know it or not, they were subjects of the Spanish Crown, tied into an imperial economy. And these changes have accelerated to the present day, binding this region ever more tightly to the rest of the world, until today we who live in the Pimería view with concern news of disease in China, war in Afghanistan, and economic collapse in Europe. And it all started with this one remarkable man, Eusebio Francisco Kino, S.J.: priest, scholar, cartographer, astronomer, and indefatigable explorer.

Father Kino founded twenty-one missions, each one in what was then an O'odham village. But herein lies a bit of confusion: founding a mission is different from building a church. It means establishing a program for the Christianization of a community, complete with church, corrals, granaries, and all the appurtenances of community life under the direction of the missionary. So when we talk of the "Kino chain of missions," we are referring to the still-living communities where Kino worked. To be sure, many of these towns still possess colonial-period churches. Few if any date from Kino's day, however. But Kino was there, he was the first to preach the Gospel there, he introduced new crops and animals to these very places. And he kept going until his death in Magdalena in March 1711.

He had ridden in to Magdalena to dedicate a new chapel to Saint Francis Xavier, and he was buried inside the chapel he had come to dedicate. And it was in that same chapel, the traces of which had been long since covered up under a later plaza, that his skeleton was discovered by an international team of archaeologists in May 1966. How this came about makes a good story: In 1961 the Arizona State Legislature selected Father Kino as the subject for one of its two representative statues in the National Hall of Statuary in Washington, D.C.

The statue was made by Baroness Suzanne Silvercruys and duly placed and dedicated in the Capitol Building. (A duplicate statue stands outside the Arizona Historical Society Museum on East Second Street in Tucson.) And then things started happening. The Mexican Ambassador reported the dedication ceremonies to the President of Mexico, who recognized that Kino was important to his country as well. Using the authority inherent in a centralized government system, the President ordered that Kino's grave be located. A binational team of archaeologists and historians was formed under the direction of Dr. Wigberto Jiménez Moreno of the National Institute of Anthropology and History, and the search was on. Documents revealed that Kino was buried in the chapel he had come to dedicate, and they told where in that chapel he was. Unfortunately, the chapel had disappeared more than a hundred years previously, and nobody knew where it had stood. After careful digging in documents and in the Sonoran earth, and a good deal of luck, the chapel foundations were located, and Kino's remains were exposed to the light once more.

The story doesn't end there. The entire main plaza of Magdalena was redesigned as a *plaza monumental,* with the church at one edge and Father Kino's grave at the other. The excavation revealing his skeleton was glassed in and covered with a dome. Inside the dome is a wonderful mural by the distinguished Sonoran painter Nereo de la Peña, showing Father Kino arriving and working in Sonora. Around the rim of the dome are listed all the missions Kino founded. And the entire town was officially renamed "Magdalena de Kino." *Finding Father Kino,* by Jorge Olvera H., is a wonderful, first-hand account of the discovery of Kino's grave.

Having said that, however, I shall continue using the shorter name of "Magdalena." For there is a lot more to be said about this fascinating place. For one thing, it is the focus of Sonora's largest and most important religious pilgrimage and fiesta, held each year in the days just prior to October 4. But hold on to your hats here—October 4 is the feast day of Saint Francis of Assisi, that medieval Italian saint who saw unity in all of God's creation, preached to the birds, embraced poverty, and founded the Order of Friars Minor, or the Franciscans. The statue that is the focus of these celebrations is an entirely different saint—the Jesuit Saint Francis Xavier, patron saint of missionaries, and Father Kino's patron. In fact, it is likely that the original statue was brought by Kino to Magdalena, to go into the chapel he dedicated on the day of his death.

Let's try to make some sense of all this. Here's how it might have happened: In 1711, Kino brings his statue of Saint Francis Xavier to Magdalena. It depicts the saint lying on his deathbed on an island off the coast of China, the next country he was planning to visit. The statue is placed in the new San Francisco chapel, which collapses and disappears over a century later, after the present church is built.

In 1767 the entire Jesuit Order—the Society of Jesus—was expelled from Spanish America due to political jealousy and maneuvering in Europe, and a few years later, the entire Society was suppressed. In Sonora, the Jesuits were replaced by Franciscans, who, as we know, had their own Saint Francis. Time moved along, as it tends to do, and in 1824 a new country—Mexico—was born out of the ashes of New Spain. For a few short years, one of Mexico's major secular holidays, for which the army could turn out and parade, was the Day of the Constitution ... October 4! All these influences seem to have come together to shift the day of the fiesta—but not its saint—to October.

More time passed. Old constitutions were shredded and new ones introduced, and October 4 was no longer a national holiday. It was still the Día de San Francisco in Magdalena, however. The Revolution of 1910 succeeded in destroying much of the Catholic Church's influence in Mexico, and by the 1930s, Sonora's government had become strongly socialist and very anticlerical. In 1935 government employees stripped many of Sonora's churches of their images, which they destroyed. Among the images to go was the reclining statue of San Francisco Xavier, the very one which might have been brought to Magdalena by Father Kino. It was hauled off to the capital city of Hermosillo, and placed in the hottest fire available—the furnaces of the Cervecería Sonora or the Sonora Brewery. But within a few years things had changed, anticlerical sentiment no longer ruled the land, and a new statue was created and placed in the chapel in Magdalena. The fiesta continues to this day, attended by thousands of pilgrims from both sides of the border. Only one detail is completely new—since the discovery of Kino's grave, the skeleton of the dead man in the plaza has come to be identified with the statue of the dead man in the church, and Magdalena's saint is now a wonderful blending of three separate historical figures: Saint Francis of Assisi, Saint Francis Xavier, and Eusebio Francisco Kino, S.J.! Just in case all this isn't sufficiently complicated, although the statue in the church is dressed in a black cassock, as a Jesuit would have been, we're not done yet. The small statues that are sold to pilgrims in the plaza wear brown Franciscan robes of a sort that were mandated for that order in the late nineteenth century.

This is a perfect example of what is called "folk religion"—all this complexity comes from the community, rather than from specialists within the official church. And if one looks a little farther, one can find many more folk elements surrounding San Francisco as he is understood in Magdalena. Take legends, for instance. The statue of San Francisco in Magdalena is neatly surrounded by a web of narratives, all of which are told as true, but which do more to reflect the hopes and beliefs of the community than they necessarily do to reveal what actually happened. One such legend is commonly told in several variations about the arrival of the statue in Magdalena. It was brought by Father Kino, I have been assured, but it was really intended for the church Kino hoped to build at San Xavier del Bac, just south of present-day Tucson. However, when the statue arrived in Magdalena, the men who were carrying it couldn't pick it up to continue the trip north. Or the axle froze on the ox cart, or the pack mule balked and wouldn't move. At any rate, the statue demonstrated emphatically that Magdalena was where it wanted to stay.

One American woman, raised on a ranch near Magdalena, told the story with a slight wrinkle: the people from San Xavier complained that the statue should be with them. "All right," said the Magdalenenses, "here it is. Come and get it!" And of course they couldn't.

Another cluster of legends surrounds the burning of the statue in 1935. Many people simply would not believe that San Francisco would allow this to happen to him. So one can still hear how the priest smuggled the statue out of the church into the hands of the faithful Tohono O'odham—The Desert People—who took it north to one of their villages. An O'odham friend told me that, according to his mother, it rained all the way on the journey, partly to confuse the "Spanish soldiers," and partly as a blessing. And sure enough, at about this time, a San Francisco statue mysteriously appeared in the O'odham village of Chuwhiy Guwsk ("Jackrabbit Falls Down"), just south of the border, near Sonoyta. Some said it was the original image from Magdalena.

Those who believe the statue to have been truly burned in the brewery furnaces in Hermosillo have stories to tell concerning what happened to the people who did the burning. The man who drove the truck carrying the statue to Hermosillo was struck and killed years later in the streets of Magdalena … by a truck from the Cervecería Sonora. A young schoolteacher who dressed a burro up in religious vestments and led it through the desecrated church became an important member of the state political system. One morning as he was being driven from Guaymas to Hermosillo, his car topped a rise and ran into a herd of burros. The car struck one and flipped it up in the air, whence it came crashing down on the car and instantly killed the passenger. Other *quemasantos* or "saint-burners," as they are called in Sonora, went mad or suffered equally terrible fates. The general message is that San Francisco pays his debts.

This theme is echoed in a multitude of stories concerning people who promised something—often to walk from Nogales to Magdalena—to the saint in return for favors rendered. If it looks as though they won't keep up their end of the bargain, San Francisco will collect in his own way, often by burning the delinquent one or some member of his or her family. San Francisco, I have been told countless times, is a miraculous saint, but he is also a saint who exacts a price … and what you owe, you must pay. This general attitude was summed up by a man who, when asked why he went on pilgrimage to visit San Francisco, replied, "To be honest, it's through fear."

In fairness, however, I must repeat the often-heard story of the man who promised to go from Cananea to Magdalena, a distance of over a hundred miles, on his knees. This he did … on a mattress in the back of a pickup truck! And any retribution on the part of the saint has never been mentioned.

Fortunately, there is a simple way to determine exactly how one stands with the saint. Almost everyone who visits the reclining statue slips a hand under its head and tries to lift it off the surface where it lies. If San Francisco allows you to raise his head, you and he are in a good relationship. If not, repairs need to be made in that relationship. And I have heard eyewitness accounts of strong men trying but failing to lift the statue, falling on their knees in prayer and weeping, and trying again, without success ... while all the time little old ladies filed by, raising the statue with one hand!

Many of these legends and beliefs apply as well to the reclining San Francisco statue that occupies the west transept of Mission San Xavier del Bac, just south of Tucson. In this case we know a little about the statue. It originally represented the Crucified Christ and could be found in the mission church at Tumacácori, halfway to present-day Nogales. When that community was abandoned due to Apache raiding in 1849, its religious statues were brought to San Xavier. Up until the early twentieth century, the Christ statue, missing its legs and one arm, lay where it lies now, apparently venerated as a Santo Entierro, or Entombed Christ. Then, sometime between 1910 and 1920, a local Franciscan priest, Father Tiburtius Wand, is said to have "recycled" it into an image of San Francisco, apparently to give the O'odham villagers a healthy alternative to their long pilgrimage to Magdalena.

I have been told that the San Xavier statue was originally in Magdalena and the Magdalena statue originally at San Xavier. After attempts at moving them to their "proper villages" failed, the two statues took on the task themselves and exchanged places. And that, I was told, was why the statue in Arizona is legless—it wore them off on the long journey! (I should have said *was* legless. During the 1990s, San Francisco was given new legs by Turkish art restorer Ridvan Isler.)

The journey to Magdalena is in fact a long, hard one, if you do as many pilgrims do and walk down from the border town of Nogales. The common practice is to go on the weekend, leaving Friday and arriving sometime Sunday, eating and sleeping on the road. "The road" in this case is International Highway 15, and in consideration of the needs of pilgrims it has a footpath beside most of its length. For the last two-thirds of the way, walking pilgrims meet up with all sorts of free help. Many people pay their vows to San Francisco by feeding the pilgrims, giving them water and simple first aid, and calling encouraging things to them. In fact, this stretch of highway becomes a very long, narrow sacred space, consecrated to San Francisco and those who walk in his honor. Everyone is friendly, everyone is helpful, and everyone is supportive. My experience has been that the more tired I get, the more I find myself floating along on the prayers and goodwill of others. In Magdalena on the feast day itself, the line to visit the saint may be several blocks long. Walkers are urged to the head of the line, pay their respects to San Francisco ... and then the party begins.

If tens of thousands of pilgrims come to Magdalena for the fiesta, more thousands come to serve their needs: toy, trinket, and religious souvenir vendors; sellers of all kinds of festive food and drink; kitchenware and blanket salespeople; musicians of all sorts, who are willing to make any party more exciting, more fun. The two plazas near the church throb with activity: mariachis, fortunetellers, norteño bands, medicine pitchmen, and Yaqui and Mayo ceremonial dancers all do their things right next to each other at the same time ... until the evening of October 4, when all of a sudden it is all over for another year.

Attendance at the fiesta is dynamic rather than static, and often reflects what is happening in the world at large. In 2001, after the destruction of the World Trade buildings in New York, there were so many pilgrims walking to Magdalena from the border that the scene resembled an actual procession. It was especially impressive after dark, with a steady stream of flashlights bobbing southward along the side of the highway. And in 2008, after reports of narcotics-related violence, the pilgrim flow dried up to a relative trickle. The Tohono O'odham Nation advertised an alternative fiesta on the American side of the border for those tribal members who did not want to risk the trip.

A good place to learn more about Magdalena and its fiesta is Chapter Three of my book, *Beliefs and Holy Places: A Spiritual Geography of the Pimería Alta.*

THE KINO MISSIONS

Father Kino founded a whole chain of missions in the Pimería Alta. Of course, the prerequisite for starting a mission program is people to missionize, and so Kino founded his institutions in already existing villages. In the centuries since his time, some of those villages have disappeared, others have remained villages, and others have grown into full-sized towns and even cities. If you hunt for Kino's first mission, Dolores, for instance, you'll find a cemetery and a monument, along with the scattered stones of a foundation. At Cocóspera, there is a lonely ruin on a hill. Átil is a village with the adobe walls of a Jesuit church, an empty 1940s church, and a large new church constructed in the 1990s. Pitiquito has a lovely Franciscan-period church in the middle of a small town, while the flourishing agricultural city of Caborca has its original mission church on the edge of town. Let's take a short look at some of the most interesting Kino missions.

The farthest east is Nuestra Señora del Pilar y Santiago de Cocóspera. The ruins of this church, romantically situated on a mesa overlooking the Río Cocóspera about twenty miles east of Ímuris, on Mexican Highway 2, may provide your only opportunity to see and touch a structure that Father Kino helped build. Actually, Cocóspera had two churches in one: a Jesuit-period adobe hall church with a door at one end and an altar at the other, and a fired brick shell dating from the Franciscan period and sandwiched around the remains of the Jesuit church. Today the church stands roofless, with its brick façade held in place by a scaffolding of steel pipe. It is under the protection of the National Institute of Anthropology and History, who pay a watchman to live in a house just below the church. A twentieth-century mortuary chapel erected by members of the prominent Elías family stands beside the ruins of the old church. The Cocóspera church, with its lovely country cemetery behind it and its grand views of the valley, makes an excellent spot for a visit or a picnic.

The pattern for the naming of mission communities in this region is usually to retain the native name for the village, adding to it the new patron saint assigned to it by the missionary. This places the village under the protection of that saint, effectively removing it from the pagan into the Christian world. In everyday speech, the community is often referred to by its native name alone, as in Cocóspera, or the places we shall visit later on in this section. San Ignacio de Cabórica, however, a village just north of Magdalena, has reversed the process and is known by its saint's name of San Ignacio. The same holds true for Santa María Magdalena, or Magdalena de Kino as it is now known.

The church at San Ignacio is a charming structure, with its original carved wooden doors, a carved plaster façade, and a spiral mesquite staircase going up the tower to the roof. Inside the sanctuary is a statue of a female saint wearing patched brown and gold robes and with her hair loose down her back. Although she is currently venerated as Santa Lucía (Saint Lucy, who is invoked for eye trouble), it seems sure that she was originally intended to represent Mary Magdalene, and was most likely smuggled out of the church at Magdalena to avoid the fiery fate that overtook the San Francisco statue in that nearby community.

Santa María Magdalena itself, in Magdalena de Kino, has a much-rebuilt nineteenth-century church. Los quemasantos were active here, and all the religious art dates from the 1940s or later. But the reclining statue of San Francisco is worth a visit, as is Father Kino's grave in the plaza. Surrounding the plaza are many shops selling sacred and secular souvenirs, as well as a small museum and a fine ice-cream parlor.

San Pedro y San Pablo de Tubutama is in the Altar River valley, west of Magdalena. The church stands parallel to the plaza, the reason for this unusual orientation probably being to make the plaza more secure against Apache attacks. The carved plasterwork on the façade and the interior make this building stand out from the others in the region. It is equipped with several interesting pieces of colonial painting and sculpture, including a really nice carved, painted, and gilded *retablo* or altarpiece dedicated to Saint Joseph.

Further down the Altar Valley is San Antonio Paduanao de Oquitoa. This lovely little rectangular hall church may be the only complete structure remaining from the Jesuit period, although the Franciscans certainly modified it slightly when they took it over. In addition to having a fine complement of colonial religious sculpture and painting, it is also the location for two of Sonora's local legends.

The first of these concerns a Franciscan priest, Father Joaquín Olizarra, O.F.M., who served the community from 1806 until his death in 1812, at the age of thirty-eight. He must have been a remarkable man, for his memory under the name of padre de las Arras is still strongly alive almost 200 years after his death. In the first place, he is said to have been a bilocator—a man who could literally be in two places at once. One day, answering a call to attend to a dying man in Tubutama, he discovered that the river ford was impassable due to heavy rains. The Indians who were with him saw him kneeling in prayer at the river bank for several hours. At the same time, people in Tubutama saw him arrive in the village, minister to the dying man, and depart. He is also said to have been able to avert deadly funnel clouds by walking out of his dwelling and making the sign of the cross at them. Finally, I have been told that his ecclesiastical superiors, disturbed by these rumors, summoned him for an interview. He arrived on a day of scattered rain and sunshine. He entered his superior's office, removed his sopping cloak, and hung it up to dry on a sunbeam! No reprimand was given that day.

The other great Oquitoa legend concerns a time around 1850 when the village was under attack by a mixed force of Seris, Papagos, and Apaches. The villagers, who were defending the church, were on the verge of running out of ammunition. Another charge might well finish them, when they observed their attackers to scatter and flee. Unexpectedly, the village was saved. Much later, a visiting Indian who had been in the hostile band gave them the explanation for their sudden flight: they had run away, he said, when they saw the relief column approaching. "What relief column?" As far as the villagers knew, no such body of soldiers had existed. "The column" said their erstwhile attacker, "that was led by the bald-headed officer in the blue cloak." Then it was clear what had happened: the village had been saved by their patron saint, San Antonio, whose image, tonsured and clad in blue Franciscan robes, stands over the altar to this day.

The late-eighteenth-century Franciscan church of San Diego del Pitiquín, in the village of Pitiquito, is unique among our churches for its teaching murals. At some point, the missionaries caused the walls to be covered with paintings—some sketchy, some finished—illustrating various points of basic Catholic doctrine. Balshazzar's handwriting on the wall from the book of Daniel, a skeleton signifying that all must die, the Virgin and a devil on opposite walls from each other, a pair of scales, the symbols of the Four Evangelists—all these could be used to illustrate sermons on the basic beliefs of Christianity. I have heard it done, by a priest whose words in Spanish were translated into English by a member of our tour group, just as they would have been translated into O'odham 200 years ago. It is still remarkably effective.

These murals were not always visible. They had been covered with white-wash throughout human memory, and it was not until 1966 that the women whose job it was to clean the church started using a detergent that started gradually dissolving this protective covering. A little girl who was sitting in Mass one day allowed her attention to wander, and noticed a drawing of a human skeleton beginning to appear on one wall. She started to scream until the whole congregation was made aware of the spectral visitor. After considerable discussion and study, many of the paintings were revealed.

Deep under even more layers of plaster, investigators found yet another set of murals. These are square frames, executed in red and white mineral paint, and appear to have been intended as frames for the Stations of the Cross. From the decorative motifs used—scallops, triangles, and snake-like figures—it seems probable that they were done by someone who possessed O'odham ritual knowledge. If this is so, these paintings are the only evidence that Native peoples took a guiding hand in the embellishment of any of their missions. This in itself is not surprising, when you consider that the purpose of the missions was to provide a setting in which native peoples could be transformed into Christian subjects of the Spanish crown.

A few miles west of Pitiquito is the thriving agricultural city of Caborca, with its mission church of La Purísima Concepción just south of the town.

The church we can see today was finished and dedicated in May 1809, and was built under the direction of Ignacio Gaona, the man responsible for San Xavier del Bac. In fact the two churches are quite similar in appearance, except for two things: the Caborca church has shorter towers and different proportions, and it was built after the final flowering of the baroque style, and so is more classical in spirit than its northern cousin. It has also had a rough life because the 1917 flooding of the Río Concepción, which runs just behind the church, took out the apse and the south transept, leaving the dome hanging miraculously over space. Repairs were made, and in the present century the church was wonderfully repaired and stabilized by a local citizens' group in time for its two hundredth anniversary.

The church at Caborca figures in Sonoran history in a way that has little to do with churches or mission history. In April 1857 the filibustering expedition of Henry Alexander Crabb arrived from California in an attempt at turning parts of Sonora into an American colony. After fighting a sharp engagement west of town, the Caborcans took refuge in the mission church, while the American besiegers occupied a thatched-roofed house across the plaza. After an unsuccessful attempt at blowing in the side door of the church on the part of Crabb's party, a relief column from the presidio (military post) at Altar arrived, led by one of popular recording artist Linda Ronstadt's ancestors. Crabb surrendered, and he, along with all but one of his followers, was summarily executed. In honor of this defense of the homeland, Caborca was formally given the epithet *heroica Caborca*, and April 6, the anniversary of Crabb's defeat, is an important local holiday.

So much for history. What remains is the folk belief that, when the Americanos tried to blow in the door of the church, they were foiled by the appearance of a Lady dressed in blue, who pinched out the burning fuse on the barrel of gunpowder. Bullets couldn't hit her, and the church door remained whole. Both Mexicans and O'odham were in the church at the time, and I have heard this story from members of both cultures. Of course the Lady in Blue was the Virgin Mary, who is often shown wearing that color. The church at Caborca belongs to her, in her guise of the Immaculate Conception. So this is our second story of a saint stepping up to defend his or her community from unbelieving outsiders.

These are the Kino missions of Sonora. In addition, there are four in Arizona: San Xavier del Bac, San José del Tumacácori, Los Santos Ángeles de Guevavi, and San Cayetano de Calabasas. San Xavier was discussed in the first chapter. The other three are included in Tumacácori National Historical Park, whose headquarters is just off Interstate 19, between Tucson and Nogales. Calabasas and Guevavi may be visited only on guided tours led by a Tumacácori Park ranger, and little remains of them except adobe walls. Tumacácori itself is another matter. It is equipped with an excellent small museum, a truly fine regional bookstore, and self-guided tours for visitors. Furthermore, it provides our only opportunity in the Pimería Alta to glimpse the mission as a functioning socioeconomic unit. Recent land acquisitions have allowed the Park to restore part of the Mission's *acequia* (irrigation ditch) system, and have permitted a wonderful project called "Father Kino's Orchard." This ongoing project has engaged a Sonoran ethnobotanist named Jesús García to locate a number of fruit trees, which appear to be descendants of plants brought by the missionaries, and to plant cuttings from them. There are several heirloom varieties of quinces, pomegranates, and even grapes already collected and planted, and their numbers are being added to as more old stock is discovered. This is indeed living, edible history!

On the first weekend of December each year, the Park is the site of the Tumacácori Fiesta, with traditional foods, crafts, music, dance, and other demonstrations from each of the groups that occupy the upper Santa Cruz Valley. This is a wonderfully low-key celebration, geared towards the community, and is well worth attending. An excellent overview of the Kino Missions and, in fact the whole Pimería Alta, may be found in *The Pimería Alta: Missions and More*, edited by James E. Officer, Mardith Schuetz-Miller, and Bernard L. Fontana.

FATHER KINO AND THE BEEF BURRO

I have mentioned that Father Kino was active in other spheres than the purely religious one. He was a cartographer, who demonstrated that California was not an island. He was also a tireless explorer, and a man who changed the face of the land he explored by introducing new crops and animals to our Pimería Alta. His most notable and long-lasting introductions were wheat and beef. As you may remember, Kino took part in mission attempts in Baja California, which failed because the new communities could not support themselves. One of his motives for crop introductions on the mainland was to create a rich supply resource for that barren peninsula. These introductions were successful to the extent that one cannot glance at the menu of a Tucson Mexican restaurant serving regional foods without having beef and wheat and their byproducts crop up over and over again.

Let's pause and consider. Over most of Mexico tortillas, those necessary adjuncts of Mexican meals, are made of corn. Here in Sonora, they are of wheat flour. Not only that, but in the Pimería Alta they have reached a tremendous size—as much as 30 inches across! If you wrap one of these giant tortillas around some sort of food, the result is called a burro. Not a "wrap." NEVER a "wrap," if we are to stay friends. (In California they make and eat things called "burritos." That is because nobody in California knows how to make the true huge, flour tortillas that one needs to create a full-sized burro.)

And what do you fill your burro with? Beef, often. Or beans. Or, if you are a teenager, peanut butter and jelly. Or you can put a slice of cheese between two small flour tortillas, toast them on the stove, and come up with a quesadilla. Or you can melt cheese on a large flour tortilla and call it a "large cheese tostada," or a "cheese crisp." But never, please, never, a "Mexican pizza." Or you can take that burro and dunk it into sizzling fat and come up with a chimichanga. (And there is a school of thought that says that the proper spelling and pronunciation is in fact chivichanga.) A lot of interesting things have been imagined and written down about the origin of this word. However, according to the dictionary of Mexicanisms, it comes from Southeastern Mexico, and roughly means "whatyoumacallit" or "thingamajig."

Here's a local story about the big flour tortillas: One day, perhaps in the 1950s, a group of visitors ordered food in a local Mexican restaurant. When the usual basket containing tortillas de harina arrived at the table, one of the men picked up a tortilla, unfolded it, and after considering the situation thoroughly, decided it was a huge napkin, and tucked it under his chin. This incident is said to have happened in at least two different restaurants: the old Lloyd's on East Sixth Street near the University Campus and the downtown El Charro Café. The latter version appears in Carlotta Flores's book, *El Charro Café,* and is told as happening in 1946 to presidential candidate Thomas E. Dewey. I first heard the Lloyd's version in the late 1950s.

By the way, the next time you travel south on Mexico's Highway 15, stop at a roadside stand in the town of Ímuris and buy a *quesadilla* or two (or three—my favorite) or maybe a *taquito de carne asada.* It isn't really true that there's a federal law that says you have to do it, but it is a wonderful way to pay respect to the memory of one of our most remarkable historical characters, Eusebio Francisco Kino, S.J. And the cheese of the quesadilla comes from the same critter as does the beef for the carne asada.

That being said, let's take a quick look at Sonoran cheese. It's all cow cheese, by the way; no sheep or goats produce cheese in Sonora, to my knowledge. Cheese comes in two basic forms: large blocks of white, fairly firm, often salty *queso blanco* (white cheese), also called *queso ranchero* or *queso regional* (ranch or regional cheese). This is good for just eating, or frying in chunks (queso *asado,* crispy on the outside and melted on the inside), or just putting in other dishes. Then there is *queso cocido* or cooked cheese, which is best for melting in quesadillas. If you travel the roads of Sonora, you'll see little roadside booths (or even hand-lettered signs on ranch gates) advertising "HAY QUESO" ("we've got cheese"). Don't be afraid to stop and try and buy. It's good stuff.

In the Magdalena and Altar valleys folks also cook down quinces (another Jesuit introduction) to make *cajeta de membrillo* or quince preserve—a wonderful, sweet, brick-like concoction that is best eaten with alternate bites of queso ranchero—a custom that came directly from eighteenth-century Spain and survives in twenty-first century Sonora. Not only can history be tasty, but time travel can be fattening!

We'll take a closer look at beef later on, but here's a preliminary glance at some of the ways Father Kino's other great introduction appears. *Carne asada* is a slice of thin-cut steak, cooked over an open fire. It's often then chopped up into tiny pieces and put into a taco or a burro. *Carne seca* ("dry beef") is beef jerky, usually seasoned with salt, chile, and garlic. Shredded up it becomes *machaca* and can then be sauteed with onions, chiles, garlic, and tomatoes. And that's enough beef for openers.

LOST MINES AND BURIED TREASURE

In his novel *The Trusty Knaves*, set in Deming, New Mexico, in the 1890s, Western author Eugene Manlove Rhodes describes a young Eastern lad sitting on the hotel porch, thinking about a story he had heard about buried Spanish treasure on the Gila River. The story came from an old prospector, and was complete with an opportunity to purchase a map. "It was a good story," comments Rhodes. "Many heads had gone into the making of it, and the years had lent it polish." Such stories as this abound in our Pimería Alta, and it is now time to take a look at some of them.

If the Southwestern borderlands may be said to be "all paved over" nowadays, it is not with cement or asphalt. It is with tales of lost mines and buried treasure. In 1977 the University of California Press published a bibliography entitled *Lost Mines and Buried Treasures of the West.* It is just a bibliography—a listing of books and articles, without any narrative or descriptive matter. The Arizona entry runs to 97 pages ... and that was in 1997. In addition, there are twenty pages on Mexico, many of which refer specifically to Sonora—which is not nearly enough. Another source for Arizona's lost mine and buried treasure tales is the forbiddingly titled *A Motif Index for Lost Mines and Treasures Applied to Redaction of Arizona Legends, and to Lost Mine and Buried Treasure Legends Exterior to Arizona,* by Byrd Howell Granger. Dr. Granger lists and gives short

Lost Virgin of Guadalupe Mine

This typical treasure map is a copy of one found inserted into a pamphlet entitled *End of a Delta* by Godfrey Sykes. A typed sheet, initialed "GWS," notes that it purports to be a map to the Virgin of Guadalupe Mine, and "a copy of a record that existed at the 'Mission of Magdalena' supposedly dated 1508–1556, and was taken to the museum at Paris, France." It should be noted that there was no mission at Magdalena in the sixteenth century, and that Paris, France, has many museums.

An engineer and hydrologist, Godfrey Sykes was an important figure in the early twentieth-century exploration of the Sonoran Desert. "GWS" was probably his son Gilbert Sykes, the great-uncle of the editor of this book, Susan Lowell Humphreys, in whose family the map remains. They consider it to be a hoax. The map was copied for Gilbert Sykes by the prominent Tucson cartographer, Don Bufkin. The beauty of the map is that it is so vague. A "vara" is an older Spanish equivalent of a yard, and pacing out yards in the country south of Tumacácori and west of the Santa Cruz River could lead one to a wide range of destinations.

synopses of every mine and treasure legend she has been able to discover, along with a complete bibliography. It is an invaluable source.

But don't get the notion that all these entries concern real, historically verified mines and treasure caches. As I suggested at the beginning of this section, folks have been making money for a long time off these stories, but not necessarily by finding the loot. Some are indeed based on what one old cowboy called a "slim foundation of fact." Americans coming into our country in the nineteenth century found abandoned mission churches, and they found old mine workings. That much is true. However, there is little evidence that the missionaries were the ones who did the mining. In fact all the documents from both the Jesuit and Franciscan periods—and there are many which give inventories of mission possessions—indicate that by the time the missionaries had paid to build their churches, fed and clothed the Indians in their care, and imported supplies from further south in New Spain, they were pretty broke. Remember, the San Xavier mission church was unfinished because the builders ran out of money. And any surplus in livestock was liable to be run off by raiding Apaches.

That didn't stop the writers and talkers from telling their stories and selling their maps, though. Some of these tales sound as though they have been, as Rhodes said, the work of many agile minds. Others quite frankly "stink of the lamp." Here's one of my favorites of the latter sort: the story of the Lost Ópata Mine.

The friars at Tumacácori had hired a group of Ópata Indians to come up and work their fabulous silver (or gold) mine. Unbeknownst to the padres, however, the chief of the Ópatas had captured a beautiful, blonde, blue-eyed Mayo princess from further south in Sonora. (It is true that some Mayos have light hair and at least gray eyes. They never had princesses, though.) But she would not submit to the Ópata's advances, so she was taken to the Chamber of Death within the mine, and tied to a stone altar table. They stripped her and smeared her all over with the deadly juice of the sotol cactus, which will cause the flesh to rot when exposed to sunlight. (There is a plant called the sotol; it is a member of the agave family. The only circumstances under which its juice can become deadly is when it is distilled into a tequila-like drink and consumed in great quantities.)

So there she was, tied to the table and smeared with sotol juice, watching the patch of sunlight from the window in the wall of the cave come closer and closer. It finally struck her, and she screamed in agony. A Franciscan passing by the window heard the screams, found the hidden chamber and the now-deceased princess, and instantly expelled the guilty Ópatas back into their Sonoran homeland. The whole mine was sealed up, complete with the bones of the princess and all the bars of gold (or silver) that had been about to be shipped. And they are all still there ...

I ran this by one of my local Mexican American friends, and asked him if he had ever heard anything like it. His reply was, "Jim, we couldn't get drunk enough to tell that one!"

Not all the stories are as juicy as this one, of course, and many may have a grain of truth to them. The fact of the matter seems to be, however, that more money has been made on lost mine scams than by finding lost mines. It is true that the northern frontier of New Spain, and later of Mexico, was an unsettled place, with Apaches raiding through every now and then. There was mineral in the ground, and money to be made by robbing payrolls. And caches of coin and other valuables have been found. So hope springs eternal ...

Unfortunately, there is a dark side to all these treasure beliefs. Treasure hunters have torn up a lot of fine desert in Arizona and Sonora. If you'll remember, the ruined mission of Cocóspera stands alone on a bluff overlooking its valley. Because it isn't in a town, it has become a natural target for treasure hunters, which is a major reason why it is in such bad shape. Great holes have been dug in the floor and knocked out of the plaster walls in a fruitless search for treasure that never was there. And there is no sign that this pernicious silliness is abating. A recently published guidebook to northern Mexico tells us, apropos of Magdalena and Father Kino's grave, that when Jesuit missionaries were buried, it was customary to bury a certain amount of silver below their graves. And folks really want to believe this rot.

One more mine should be mentioned—the Lost Virgin of Guadalupe Mine, said to be somewhere near Tumacácori. This story is supported by at least one "ancient manuscript" which exists today in several versions. One of these is known as the "Sister Micaela Molina Document." In 2006 the National Park Service (which administers Tumacácori National Historic Park) posted in detail the evidence that leads it to believe that the document is a twentieth-century hoax. In the long discussion that followed on the Internet, many believers in the lost mine accused the Park Service of faking the evidence because the government wanted to keep the treasure for itself! And the search goes on.

According to Granger's précis, the mine was worked "by the Indians" at Tumacácori from 1508 to 1648. It was seized in 1540 by the explorer Coronado. Coronado constructed a mission and named the mine for the "patron saint of Mexico." There is no evidence that Coronado ever made it to the Santa Cruz Valley, and there is little documentary evidence for the devotion to Guadalupe anywhere in Mexico before the seventeenth century. Nevertheless, the mine, which is said to contain 2,050 mule loads of silver and 905 loads of gold, remains a favorite target for treasure hunters.

Two excellent articles debunking the majority of lost mine stories are "Legends of Lost Missions and Mines," by Charles W. Polzer, S.J., and "Ravaged Ruins: The Destruction of Our Cultural Heritage," by William W. Wasley.

Of course legendary buried treasure doesn't happen only in lost mines and mythically wealthy missions. This was a pretty unstable part of the world, what with bandits, Apaches, and other energetic parties, and so, the stories tell us, there might be buried gold anywhere. Under the fireplace in an old house, for instance, where the owners had left it for safekeeping … and never returned. Or just about anywhere else. The supernatural world has its little ways to communicate this sort of information: mysterious lights or glows on the ground, or maybe on a cactus or tree. One could find just about anything in the desert after dark.

Sometimes what one finds isn't exactly what one was looking for. A man riding through the desert once found a tiny baby lying on the ground. Of course he picked it up to take it back home. As he was riding along he noticed that the baby was smiling at him … and had long, pointed teeth. It was the devil. The man dropped the baby and galloped off towards home. According to the story, he was pretty shy of babies for the rest of his life.

Allied to the lost mission mine stories are the tunnel tales. Every mission church in the area seems to have its story about a secret tunnel, leading, perhaps, to whatever river happens to be nearby. Here the missionaries could hide when rebellion overtook them. And here the fabulous golden treasures of the church could be stored away. The only problem is, no real record of any such tunnel has been found. I have been told that the citizens of Tubutama, in the 1940s, surprised a group of Americans who were on the verge of dynamiting the entire church to get at the treasure tunnel. Did that really happen, or is it another aspect of the ubiquitous buried treasure legends, this time from another point of view? I really don't know.

What I do know is that the stories are here, all around us: the Mine of the Iron Door, El Tejano, the Lost Guadalupe Mine, the Silver Bells of Tumacácori ... and many, many more. I also know that there are few regional pleasures to beat sitting under a ramada on a summer evening when it's too hot to sleep, and the summer lightning storms chase each other across the valley, and listening to the slow unwinding of one of these tales. And that is the real treasure.

VOICES FROM INSIDE A LARGE, BLACK SNAKE

In May 1999 I was photographing roadside crosses along Highway 15 south of Santa Ana, Sonora. A young man was cutting grass for his horse along the side of the road, and I explained to him what I was doing, remarking that a lot of people seem to have died along that stretch of highway. He replied, "My grandmother told me that when she was a little girl a big black snake came to Sonora and started eating people. And it was the highway." What can we learn, listening to the voices from the black snakes on both sides of the border?

In the first place, a lot of people have died along our roads, trails, and highways. The custom of erecting a cross to mark the site of a sudden death—the place where a soul was separated from its body without any of the preparation afforded by the Catholic church—is as old as the European presence in Mexico. In 1783 the primary cause of sudden death was the Apaches. Fray Antonio de los Reyes, the first Bishop of Sonora, entreated the Spanish civil authorities to forbid the erection of such monuments, because they struck fear into the hearts of the travelers, profaned the sacred symbol of the cross, and added to the boldness and arrogance of the Apaches. You will be happy to know that the practice was duly forbidden. A drive through present-day Sonora will suggest how effective this ban was.

These death marker crosses are in fact interactive signals; they are supposed to elicit a response. According to Catholic belief, a person who dies without the last rites of the Church has probably ended up in Purgatory, a place of purification and cleansing. He or she may be helped onward by the prayers of the living. So the crosses can serve as reminders to passersby to say a prayer for the deceased. In the old days, when travel was by horse or foot, the cross would often surmount a pile of rocks. The traveler could leave a small stone on the pile, in addition to any prayers he or she wished to say. These rock-pile shrines also used to be placed at potentially dangerous places, like river fords, and seem to have been in use long before the Spaniards brought Christianity into this region.

The simplest and most common form of roadside death marker is the cross. Crosses sometimes are inscribed with the name and dates of the deceased. Often small unsalvageable pieces of the wrecked car—broken glass, chrome stripping, floor pads, and the like—are placed on the ground next to the cross. Sometimes in place of a cross there is a small freestanding niche or *nicho*, often containing a saint's image. Sometimes an entire *capillita* or small chapel is erected, of either single- or double-phone booth size. In cases such as these a photograph of the deceased person may well hang on the wall or stand on the altar.

Related in form are the roadside chapels that are not death memorials but rather commemorate an apparent miracle. Someone may fall ill, and a family member may promise a specific saint to erect a chapel if the loved one recovers. Such a vow is called a *manda*, and is similar to a promise made to San Francisco to walk to Magdalena, for instance. Some of these chapels are well known and have long and wonderful stories attached to them. Take, for example, the chapel to San Ramón (Saint Raymond) on the east side of Highway 15 as it leaves Nogales, Sonora.

In the 1930s that was open country, and when their daughter experienced difficulty in childbirth, the owners of a nearby ranch promised San Ramón a small chapel if mother and child survived. (Saint Raymond, himself the product of an emergency caesarian operation, is usually asked for help with birthing problems.) So the chapel was built. When I first saw it, it was quite a ways out of town near a mesquite grove where local buses would stop and rest before their journey back north. The chapel had acquired a reputation as an appropriate place at which to stop, light a candle, and say a prayer at the beginning or ending of a long trip, like the drive to Hermosillo.

Time passed, and Nogales expanded in the postwar years. The hill where the chapel was built has been given over to huge maquiladoras or duty-free assembly plants, which in their turn have attracted thousands of people from other parts of Mexico to their potential jobs. And one of the plants was built with its street-side wall cutting through the site of the chapel. However, every time the wall would go up, it would collapse. The third time it did this one of the men in charge of construction was killed. So a compromise was reached. The chapel was reconstructed, with the wall going around it, leaving it open to the street. It is larger than it was before, but still dedicated to San Ramón.

Then new stories started to be told. It was said that some people (and it was implied that they were uncivilized recent arrivals) were in the habit of stealing a statue of San Ramón from the chapel and praying to him in their own homes. If their prayers were answered, they would buy a replacement statue for the chapel. If not, they would knock the old statue's head off and toss it into the chapel door. I have never heard any proof that this shocking custom actually exists, but I have certainly heard stories to that effect. I suspect this modern legend is really about the discomfort old-time Nogales residents feel with the huge population increases of the last decades.

Of the many roadside chapels and shrines in northern Sonora, some have stories that connect them with the drug trade. Truckers on the highways have told me of certain shrines and religious murals that were paid for by prominent narcotraficantes. These all seem to be on northbound highways. And then there are the chapels dedicated to *la santísima Muerte*—Most Holy Death—which have appeared within the past few years on the highways just south of Nogales and Agua Prieta. La Santa Muerte is represented as a grinning skeleton, often holding a scythe in one hand and a globe in the other. She seems to be traditionally involved in spells and witchcraft, and often—but not exclusively—with people who operate on the far side of the law. In December 2008 there was a cluster of five chapels dedicated to her a few miles south of Nogales, Sonora. By early January of 2009, all the statues in those chapels had been decapitated or removed. By April of the same year, two statues had had their heads replaced, while others remained "wounded." And in March of that same year, Tucson newspapers reported that authorities in Nuevo Laredo, in the northeastern Mexican state of Tamaulipas, had, with the help of an army escort, bulldozed some thirty of her chapels in that city. So the pattern goes. Ancient customs and traditions are put to use serving highly contemporary ends.

More information on Sonora's roadside religious monuments may be found in my articles, "Voices from Inside a Black Snake: Religious Monuments of Sonora's Highways" and "Voices from Inside a Black Snake, Part II: Sonoran Roadside Capillas."

Now it's time to leave religious history and lore for a while, and go out into the desert.

CHAPTER FOUR

Desert Wanderings

LET'S START THIS PHASE OF OUR JOURNEY with the folks who most legitimately call the Sonoran Desert "home"—the Tohono O'odham or "Desert People." Long before this region was part of something called "the Southwest," and long before Father Kino set out to convert the Upper Pimas, the Desert People were here. In those days, outsiders called them "Papagos"—a name taken from a word meaning "bean eaters." Late in the twentieth century, the Papagos returned to what they have always called themselves—"O'odham," or The People. To distinguish themselves from the People who live by the Salt and Gila Rivers, they added "Tohono" to their name. They are not just "Desert People" but "*The* Desert People." In their eyes, they have always lived here. It is to this place that I'itoi, their Creator and Elder Brother, led them up out of the Underworld. Here is where Baboquivari, their sacred mountain, stands. Here is where they were living during those times that can only be reached through sacred stories. Here they were living when the Spaniards arrived, here they were living when an international border was thrust through the middle of their homeland, and here they live today. They are the Tohono O'odham, the Desert People.

Closely related are the Akimel O'odham, the River People, who dwelt, and still dwell, by the Gila and Salt rivers north of Tucson. They have a similar language and similar customs, and share many of the same stories explaining how things are and the way in which things came to be. They never had Spanish missions in their midst, however, so the overlay of Spanish Catholicism is not as strong among them.

When the missionaries arrived, the Tohono O'odham had worked out three different patterns of living, depending upon the availability of water. The "one-village" people lived next to year-round rivers like the San Pedro and the Santa Cruz, where they were able to irrigate their crops. Of the O'odham in what is now Arizona and Sonora, these were the ones who had the first and heaviest contact with Europeans. All too soon, they were decimated by new diseases for which they had no built-up immunity. The native population shrunk, villages were abandoned, and Desert People sometimes moved in to fill up the ranks.

Further west lived the "two-village" people, who moved back and forth on a seasonal basis. During the winter months they would live near some permanent source of water—a sandstone tank or a dripping spring—in the foothills. In the summer rainy season, they would move down into the flats, where they would practice a sophisticated form of floodplain irrigation. The rains over and crops harvested, they would move back up to the winter villages. This was the pattern practiced over what is now the big Tohono O'odham Reservation. Over the course of the twentieth century, deep wells have been drilled in all the villages, and most O'odham have moved permanently into their summer homes, to take advantage of good roads for the school bus.

Finally, in the far west, towards the Gulf of California, lived the "no-village people" in a land so dry that it could not support a permanent, sedentary population. These Hia Ced O'odham or "Sand People" moved in small bands, hunting and gathering wild crops. The Sand People remain, but their ancient territories are empty and their traditional ways of making a living have gone.

The O'odham have preserved what seems to be the oldest body of stories connected with this place. They are lovely, long, complex, and allusive rather than descriptive. Furthermore, there are certain times of year—the hot months when the lightning comes and the snakes are out—when they should not be told. When one deals with the printed page, this stricture becomes impossible, of course. However, the stories are not my stories, and respect must be shown to their owners. So I will try to honor the old rules to some extent by writing *about* them, rather then retelling them in detail. Is this hair-splitting a legacy of Father Kino and his Jesuit education? I don't know, but it seems to be a workable compromise.

The stories concern I'itoi, the Creator and Elder Brother of the Tohono O'odham. After creating people and leading them up from the Underworld, I'itoi retired to a cave on the west side of Baboquivari Mountain, that dramatic peak to the southwest of Tucson. (Its O'odham name is *Waw kiwulk* or "Constricted Rock.") There he stayed, and there, according to many O'odham, he still is. On certain occasions, when the People of the Desert were in serious trouble, I'itoi would come out and help.

On one of these occasions, a huge, whale-like animal called a *ñehbig* was occupying the area near present-day Organ Pipe Cactus National Monument. It was sucking things into itself—plants, animals, people, even whole villages. The People asked I'itoi for help, and he told them to gather a certain kind of black rock, cut four long poles of greasewood, and wait for him. Although he had looked like a little old man when they visited him in his cave, he arrived as a strong, young fellow. Armed with the black rocks and the poles, he allowed himself to be sucked into the ñehbig. As he went down its throat, he propped it open with the poles. Arriving at the creature's heart, he used the black rocks, which might have been obsidian, to cut out that organ, and then escaped before the monster's throat collapsed. In one version of the story, in its death throes the ñehbig thrashed all the water out of the lake it had been living in. Occasional finds of large fossil bones in the area have been identified by many O'odham as ñehbig bones.

On another occasion, O'odham living in the village of Pozo Verde, just south of the Mexican border near present-day Sasabe, were troubled by an individual called Ho'ok, who was living in a nearby cave and stealing and eating village children. Once again, I'itoi was asked for help. He told the villagers to have a dance, invite Ho'ok, and give her special cigarettes to make her sleepy. The dance lasted for four days and nights, by the end of which time Ho'ok became very sleepy. The people carried her to her cave in the south end of the Baboquivari Mountains, and filled the cave with firewood. They then set the wood on fire and sealed the entrance to the cave. Ho'ok perished in the fire. Villagers at Pozo Verde can still show the cave and the location of the dance ground.

This is just the center part of a long story which starts with how Ho'ok came to be, and goes on to tell how bits of her which escaped burning went on to cause more damage. But even in its shortened form the story should serve as a sort of title to the land for the O'odham. Their stories reach farther back then anyone else's, tie them more intimately to this desert place. As one O'odham musician friend said when I introduced his band to an audience, "We hope you make us welcome, because after all we made you welcome."

One further place on Tohono O'odham Nation deserves mention. This is the shrine to the Flood Children, one of the desert's sacred places. It is near the village of Santa Rosa, and permission should be asked at the Santa Rosa District office before one visits it. It consists of a circle of peeled ocotillo stalks, bending outwards. There is a gap in the circle for each of the cardinal directions. In the center of the circle is a small pile of rocks. The story goes that one morning, in that corner of time that is only approachable through oral tradition, a farmer chased a badger that was eating his beans and melons. The badger went into his hole, and the farmer dug after him. All of a sudden, out of the hole gushed, first a high wind, and then an endless stream of water. It was obvious that the whole world was in danger of being flooded, and so medicine men came to the site to deliberate what should be done to stop the flow. The men put different animals down the hole, but the flood did not really stop. Finally it was realized that four children, a boy and a girl from each of the two main divisions of the Desert People, were needed to take the message to the Underworld. The children were selected, dressed in special clothes, painted in special ways, and taken to the hole. As the elders sang, the children danced in place, and slowly sank down. They are there now, many O'odham believe, not dead but living in the Underworld. Once every four years when the materials on the shrine are renewed, the Flood Children come back and dance to the singing of the People. Nobody actually sees them, but the People know they are there.

There are many stories connected with the Flood Children, but one of the loveliest is this. After the children had arrived in the Underworld, I'itoi took them on a journey to show them the beauty of the world they had helped save. They went to the shore of the Gulf of California, where the Children ran through the water, skipping and kicking up foam, with the sea birds flying over their heads. If you ever go to Tucson Meet Yourself or some similar event that features traditional O'odham dancing, you will probably see a dance called the *chelkona* or the "Skipping and Scraping Dance." It is done by a line of young men and a line of young women with their faces painted white. The boys carry effigies of birds, while the girls carry white triangles representing clouds. The two lines dance in parallel, cross each other, weave in and out to the tones of singing and rattling. The dance commemorates this moment of joy, of sacrifice, of the revelation of beauty.

Among the River People, the Elder Brother figure is known as Se'e'e. Many of the stories concerning him, however, are essentially the same as they are among the Desert O'odham. After leading the People out of the Underworld, he retired to his house in a mountain and emerges in times of great need to help his people. The ubiquitous Man in the Maze basket design (also known to the Tohono O'odham as I'itoi Ki or I'itoi's House) is said on one level to refer to a house he made for himself where he would be safe from his enemies. On another level, it is a road that each person must travel in his or her life.

There is a large body of literature on both the Desert and the River People. Here are some good places to start, with particular emphasis on the traditional stories:

Of Earth and Little Rain by Bernard L. Fontana, with photographs by John P. Schaefer, provides an excellent look at the Tohono O'odham as they were in the late twentieth century. *The Desert Smells Like Rain: A Naturalist in Papago Indian Country* by Gary Paul Nabhan approaches the same people in terms of their relationship to their desert land. *O'odham Hoho'ok A'agitha: Legends and Lore of the Pima and Papago Indians* by Dean and Lucille Saxton is an excellent introduction to O'odham oral literature. Finally, *The Short, Swift Time of Gods on Earth* by Donald Bahr, Juan Smith, William Smith Allison, and Julian Hayden, gives us a version of the complete Akimel O'odham creation narrative, collected in 1935.

Every Tohono O'odham village possesses at least one Catholic chapel. Some go so far as to have two: a church built by Franciscan missionaries in the twentieth century, and a smaller chapel which is devoted to the particularly O'odham form of Catholicism called *santo himdag* or "saint way." The O'odham learned this religious system in the eighteenth and nineteenth centuries, mostly by watching their Mexican neighbors. It involves the building of chapels in which to store powerful sacred images, and the holding of feasts and processions and dancing at certain times of the year. In its outward manifestations, santo himdag seems quite Catholic. In reality, it is a wonderful adaptation of Catholic behaviors into a basically O'odham system, which is designed to maintain the physical, mental, and spiritual health of the community. Let's follow an O'odham family as they make their traditional pilgrimage to Magdalena, mentioned in Chapter Three.

After arriving in Magdalena, they may purchase ribbons to symbolize the fulfillment of their pilgrimage, and quite possibly a saint's statue or holy picture. The latter might well be purchased from one of the craftspeople who encase standard holy cards into reverse-painted glass frames. These frames are unique to Magdalena, and are available only at fiesta time. A design, complete with painted framing lines, is painted in both translucent and opaque colors on the back of a small sheet of glass. A backing of sheet tin or cardboard is covered with crumpled aluminum foil, and then a commercially produced holy card bearing the picture of a saint is slipped under the glass, into the painted frame. Then glass and backing are attached to each other. The crumpled foil produces a wonderful, glittering effect behind the translucent paint.

The artists who produce these painted frames belong to a class locally known as *pajareros,* or "bird catchers." They pursue a number of different ways of making a living, trapping and selling wild songbirds, making bird traps and cages, harvesting wild crops, collecting and selling medicinal herbs, and operating booths at local religious and arts festivals. One pajarero, the late Anastacio León, became a regular participant in Tucson Meet Yourself and the Tumacácori Fiesta, and participated in the Smithsonian Festival of American Folklife in Washington, D.C.

The images will be taken into the chapel where San Francisco's statue rests, and either rubbed on the statue or left for a while with the statue, so as to absorb some of the vast power inherent in that image. Then the card or small statue will be taken back to the Reservation, to the purchaser's village. After being blessed with holy water to align its new power with the power and needs of the village, it is stored in the chapel where it helps protect the people and animals of the village.

O'odham chapels almost always face east, and usually stand within a fenced or cleared dirt churchyard. To the east of this is a cross, around which processions pass on feast days. Inside the churchyard are a dance floor of dirt or cement, a small three-sided house for the band to play in, an outdoor kitchen and bread oven, and a dining area. All these come into play during the feast days, which often start off with a late-morning procession. After the procession, the feeding starts. A steer is slaughtered, and all comers are fed in shifts, all afternoon and through the night until around dawn. A typical O'odham feast includes beef stew with the bones left in the pot, beef and red chile stew, possibly enchiladas, beans, potato salad, fresh-baked bread, and tortillas. Dessert is usually cake and/or Jell-O. The meal may be washed down with coffee and a non-alcoholic fruit punch. And if you haven't experienced the joys of eating red-hot red chile, calmed down with potato salad and eaten with home-baked bread or a huge flour tortilla, you have a real regional treat in store for you.

Around dusk the music starts. What you hear at these occasions is a special kind of O'odham music called *waila,* a word derived from the Spanish *baile,* or "social dance." Waila consists of polkas, two-steps, and *cumbias,* played on button accordion, saxophone, electric guitar, electric bass, and drum kit. Descended from an older style of music played on violins, guitars, bass drum, and snare drum, waila music came to the O'odham at some time in the middle of the nineteenth century and has been going strong ever since. There is always a waila band at the Tucson Meet Yourself festival, and the music had an entire annual Waila Festival in Tucson dedicated to it until the economic crisis of 2009. There are high hopes that this wonderful event, which was revived in the fall of 2010, will continue on an annual basis.

The Tohono O'odham are the most active basket-making tribe in the United States, and their lovely work can be seen in Native arts stores all over the country. Other crafts include pottery making, jewelry making, and genre painting.

LA CORUA AND HER FRIENDS

Lying dimly in the background of all we have discussed so far in this chapter is an animal called in Spanish *la corua.* In ordinary Sonoran Spanish, a "corua" is a boa constrictor. The Corua, however, is something different, according to the oldest generation of Spanish-speaking country people. It is the big snake that lives in springs and other bodies of still water and protects them. Some say it has long fangs with which to clean underground veins of water, some say it has a smooth mouth and a cross on its forehead. If you kill the corua, its spring dries up. If one pursues this connection between water and snakes, as my friend Richard Morales and I did several years ago, you'll find that the vocabulary of snakes and the vocabulary of irrigation in this part of the world are surprisingly similar to each other. As I put it at one point, "Every time we start looking at snakes we get our feet wet, and every time we follow an irrigation ditch we end up with a snake by the tail." While many Native peoples in our borderlands have Water Serpent stories, none of these stories exhibit more than a haunting, shadowy resemblance to each other. For instance, the ñehbig thrashed all the water out of the lake in its death throes. Is this a corua story, or a coincidence?

Corua, by the way, is a loan word from Yaqui, and *co* is a root signifying "snake" in several languages of the Uto-Aztecan family, of which Yaqui and O'odham are members. Remember Quetzal*co*atl, the famed Aztec feathered serpent? Is our corua some relative of that powerful beast, living in the memories of Mexican vaqueros? Good questions, to which as yet we have no answers. But there it is, coiled in our water holes like a giant question mark. And, as Richard Morales remarked, "If you kill the corua, you lose your water rights." The corua is discussed more fully in Chapter Two of *Beliefs and Holy Places*.

The corua appears to come to us from the Native American past. Not so, perhaps, three other animals whose existence is believed in but which are seldom seen by outsiders. The *carabunco* is known in northern Sonora, and especially in the Altar Valley. It is either a bird-like or a lizard-like creature, seen only at night, and distinguishable by the bright jewel-like light that shines in the middle of its forehead. It often flies over places where there is a lot of gold buried, either in the form of treasure or in a natural deposit. Although it sounds both familiar and European, I have been able to find no specific old-world analogues for it. There has been a belief, lasting from Greek through medieval times that a stone called the carbuncle grows under the horn of a unicorn, and may be used in the healing of wounds. Vague though this is, it is worth mentioning.

The *chupacabras* ("goatsucker"), on the other hand, provides a wonderful example of media-fueled contemporary folklore. At some point in the early 1990s, Puerto Ricans noticed that they occasionally found the bodies of goats and chickens emptied of blood. From this came the idea of the chupacabras. The media got hold of it and decided that it must be a sinister visitor from outer space. Then it was sighted in Mexico. For a few months, nobody could talk of anything else ... and then it headed for the international border! A man in Douglas, Arizona, saw one, and then a man in Tucson chased one out of his son's bedroom. The wonderful thing about this critter was that everyone responded to it in different ways. Some folks were genuinely frightened. Others saw opportunities for fame and/or fortune. One man in Mexico City walked around in a homemade wire mesh cage, hoping to get a photograph of it. Casts of chupacabras footprints were hawked on the Internet. A restaurant in Mexico City advertised a chupacabras sandwich, saying little definite about it except that it contained a lot of catsup. A norteño band in California recorded a song that explained that the chupacabras was actually a Martian from the moon, who came to earth and sucked blood in an attempt to cure a monstrous hangover. He is no longer a source of danger, we were told, because he has discovered love ... but he leaves terrible hickeys! Finally, Mexico's ever-active political satirists put the word around that the chupacabras was really ex-president Salinas de Gortari, who had sucked Mexico dry through the corruption of his administration. Something for everyone, indeed!

Chupacabras T-shirts appeared for sale, some emphasizing the President Salinas connection, some celebrating the beast's Puerto Rican origins. For a while these were readily available at Tucson's Tanque Verde Swap Meet. One friend brought me a small plastic bottle in the shape of a chupacabras, in which soft drinks had been sold in Chihuahua City. Then the craze slowed down and stopped.

One curious point remains to be mentioned concerning the chupacabras: when faced with the same phenomenon of blood-drained livestock, Mexicans and Puerto Ricans postulate a visitor from outer space, while Anglo-Americans prefer to believe in hidden Satanic cult followers practicing their abominable secret rites. And that is something to think about—The Enemy Without versus The Enemy Within. Chupacabras can be readily identified, so the stories tell us ... but Satanists might be the folks next door, and one would never know. A good recent book on the chupacabras is *Tracking the Chupacabras: The Vampire Beast in Fact, Fiction, and Folklore,* by Benjamin Redford.

Sobering up slightly, we can't leave the subject of legendary critters without taking a look at the *onza,* a big cat, like a mountain lion but fiercer, that some people believe occupies the Sierra Madre of western Mexico. It is almost indistinguishable from a cougar (or puma or mountain lion), and in fact, that is what it probably is. But since colonial times some writers and storytellers and hunters have maintained that there are three big cats in the Sierra—*el león* (mountain lion), *el tigre* (jaguar), and la onza. Photos have been compared, skulls and hides collected, tests made, and books written. For believers, the case remains open. There actually is an impartial book on the onza. It's *Onza! The Hunt for a Legendary Cat,* by Neil Carmony.

Now we pass from animals that are believed in by different groups of people to animals that were created for the purposes of deception, pure and simple. We have already entered the realm of the tall tale or "windy" in Chapter One with the sand trout. Here are a few more imaginary beasts that primarily serve to confusticate the newcomer. Before we start, I'd like to retell a story my friend Joe Harris tells as a personal experience. He was standing downtown when a woman tried to use a public scale—the sort that gives one's weight and "fortune" in exchange for a small coin. She was carrying an armload of packages, and couldn't see the scale around them. Joe offered to hold her parcels for her, tucking one of them under his arm. After she had thanked him, collected her possessions, and left, Joe realized that he still had one of her packages under his arm. He tried to find its owner, but couldn't. After he finally got home, he decided to open the wrapped object.

The story seemed to end there, so after waiting for a very short time, I predictably asked what was in the package. Joe's reply: "Fish hooks to catch suckers like you!" And that sets the stage very nicely indeed for the next few stories.

If I'm taking a visitor on a walk in the desert, I am fairly likely to find a stick, a little thinner than a standard pencil and from six to eight inches long. "Well," I may remark, "I haven't seen one of those for a long time." My guest, if he or she has any natural curiosity at all, will take the hook and ask what it is. "Why," I say, "it's a lizard stick. Haven't you heard of the Sonoran Desert stick lizards?" Then I go on to explain that they are just like other lizards, except that they have tender feet, and carry sticks like this around with them. When the sun starts getting really hot in the middle of the day, they jam the stick into the sand, climb up it, and perch on top of it till the shadows lengthen and the ground cools off. Some people also claim that they keep cool by sitting in their own shadows, but I personally think that's an exaggeration.

An old gunsmith of my acquaintance named Lou Welker used to tell about the pelicannon, a bird that lived on the mud flats at the head of the Gulf of California. It had springy tail feathers, big paddle feet, and a fifty-caliber hole at the end of its beak, which in all other details resembled that of the common pelican. With its feet it would roll mud balls, dry them in the sun, and store them in its beak. It would then sneak up on its prey, stun it with a mudball fired from its beak, and absorb the recoil on its tail feathers. Digging a hole in the ground with its feet, it would shove the prey in and whip it to a froth with its huge feet. It would suck the resulting liquid up through its hollow beak. Some bird! I haven't heard any recent reports concerning pelicannon sightings, so they may have become extinct.

So far we have dealt with evolutionary adaptations to the slow process of natural change. The desert dries out, and sand trout grow lungs rather than gills. Stick lizards moving onto our burning sands learn to use lizard sticks. But within the past hundred years, humans have caused monumental changes in the hitherto natural environment. Has our regional wildlife responded to these changes in any way? You bet it has, according to a Xeroxed handout sheet that bears the imprint of either the Department of the Interior or the Bureau of Reclamation. I have lost the paper, so I can't remember which. It doesn't really matter, however, for I suspect that neither of those august governmental bodies was in fact responsible for the document in question, which circulated informally from hand to hand. Stay tuned for the amazing story of *Myotis digitalis*, the long-thumbed bat of Lake Powell.

It seems that after the Glen Canyon Dam was constructed and Lake Powell started to fill up, the colonies of bats that lived in the caves along what was rapidly becoming the lakeshore found themselves threatened. Their caves started to flood, and soon the entrances were submerged beneath the waters of the new lake. This was a slow process, however, and the high ceilings in many of the caves did not make them uninhabitable for the bats, as only the entrances were under water. So the bats learned to swim—sometimes as far as twenty-five feet or more, to the surface of the lake and back again, on their usual evening-to-morning schedule. Over several generations, these bats developed unusually long thumbs with which they would plug their nostrils on the long, wet journey. The helpful minibrochure goes on to suggest that tourists wishing a glimpse of these bats should drive slowly along the shores of Lake Powell, looking for tiny towels on the sand.

Now if anyone objects to this sort of gentle deception, remember that there is strong precedent in the Bible, where it says, "I was a stranger and you took me in."

Unfortunately there's nothing fictional about mosquitos. However, in the desert environment they can grow to a great size. I have been told that two of them cornered an old prospector up Wickenburg way, threatening him to the extent that he was forced to hide under a huge overturned ore bucket. Soon he heard a tapping noise and realized that the mosquitos were drilling through the top of the bucket to get at him. He took his rock hammer and clinched their beaks over once they got through, whereupon they flew away with the bucket. And I have heard reliable reports that in the 1950s a mosquito landed at Luke Air Force Base near Phoenix, and they filled it up with high-octane fuel before they realized that it had the wrong markings on its wings.

Not only are our desert fauna subject to a certain degree of artistic license, but so are our meteorological phenomena. It gets so dry here sometimes that the trees follow the dogs around and you have to prime the old men before they can spit. The west wind blows so hard in the summertime that the sun sets three hours late. Owners of chickens must take care that their hens don't get backed the wrong way into the wind, or they'll lay the same egg over and over again. One pitiful sight around our house was our old family dog wandering around the place at midnight, looking for a little shade to lie down in. Cows have been known to lie on their backs when it gets really hot in June and July and give themselves milk baths. In fact when it *really* gets hot, you can drop an egg on the pavement and it will be hard cooked before it breaks. The standard code term for when Tucson's temperatures finally hit 100 degrees (in May of this year!) is that the ice is breaking on the Santa Cruz River. In more light-hearted days, this phenomenon would be reported in detail and with a straight face in the Tucson dailies. I was once told in Yuma that the speaker knew it was starting to warm up (the temperature was at around 110 that day) because the snow was beginning to melt on the north sides of the saguaro cactus. And so we make light of what we need to put up with. The implication is, of course, that it takes a certain especially tough sort of person to live here.

CHAPTER FIVE

Riding the Grub Trail

THIS CHAPTER DEALS WITH A SUBJECT that is dear to my heart—food. And that's not just because I like to eat, either. By looking at traditional food-ways—the selection, preparation, uses, and meanings of food in a cultural context—one can learn a lot about the culture and region under consideration. Let's start with the wild foods that still can be found, gathered, and eaten in the Sonoran Desert.

WILD FOOD

Our tall, columnar cacti, the saguaros and the pitahaya or organ pipe cactus, bear fruit in early summer, and in each case the fruits are sweet to munch on and wonderful when boiled down into syrup or jellies. Saguaro harvesting is still an important O'odham seasonal occupation. It is accomplished with a special tool called a *guiput*. (Sorry, but I've never heard an equivalent in English or Spanish.) A guiput consists of two saguaro ribs lashed end to end, and a small diagonal crosspiece of the same material at one end. (For low-growing fruit or very tall people, the gardening tool called a "hula hoe" serves very well ... but you miss most of the high-growing fruit that way. After all, saguaros can grow to well over thirty feet tall.) You select the fruit that are starting to turn pink at the base, knock them off with the crosspiece, and put them in a bag or bucket. If you wait until the fruit is pink all over, or until it opens at the top, you'll find that the birds have beaten you to it. Saguaro fruit can be eaten just as it is, or boiled to make a syrup or even a jelly. The Tohono O'dham ferment the syrup into a weak cactus wine, which is used in traditional rain-attracting ceremonies. And by the way, according to many O'odham, saguaros are people. One should not shoot at them, throw rocks at them, or submit them to any sort of painful or disrespectful treatment.

Pitahayas present a different problem. If you knock their fruit down, it will shatter, so a pitahaya picking stick carries a blade at its end to slice the fruit from the cactus, and just above the blade is a nail with which to transfix the fruit so it doesn't drop. It's worth the bother, though, as pitahaya fruit is full of sugar, and eats very well indeed. Prickly pear fruit should be picked with tongs, and it makes fine jellies. Even the cholla, that most stickery of all cacti, has flower buds that may be harvested, cleaned of spines, boiled, and turned into a nice salad. But please use tongs for this job.

Chiltepines are tiny, round, wild chiles. There are a few stands in southern Arizona, one of which, in the Tumacácori Mountains, is an official preserve for these fiery little fruits. They may be eaten green, allowed to ripen and eaten red, or dried. In the latter case, they may crumbled onto one's food with the fingers (as Father Ignatz Pfefferkorn observed in the mid-eighteenth century), or pounded in a small mortar. These mortars are usually made of ironwood or mesquite wood, and are most easily available at fruit and vegetable stands along the old highway through Magdalena, Sonora.

But watch out with chiltepines, though. They are fiery hot—the word "spicy" is insufficiently strong to use in connection with them. In fact I have been told that the birds who live near the chiltepín preserve in the Tumacácoris and eat the chiltepines (thus spreading their seeds) are the only birds in the world who habitually fly backwards into a high wind.

In the summer, after the rains have come, wild greens will sprout up in fields, vacant lots, and beside roads. Two in particular, verdolagas (pigweed) and quelites (wild amaranth) are often gathered, cooked, and eaten by O'odham and Mexicans. They can be treated like any greens and sauteed up with some onion, or added to salads. While they last, they are a welcome addition to the local diet.

A good introduction to these ancient wild food plants is *Gathering the Desert* by Gary Paul Nabhan.

Wild foods aside, this chapter concentrates on the foods one can find in regional restaurants in southern Arizona and northern Sonora. I say "regional" because Mexican food, like Mexico itself, is highly regional. What Mexican restaurants in Southern Arizona serve is indeed "Mexican" food, but it's actually "Sonoran food prepared for American tastes." However, if you go to California, New Mexico, or Texas, you will find different dishes, different combinations, different flavors. And that is even truer when you move south of the border.

TORTILLAS

Let's start with the lowly tortilla. We are told that when the great Moctezuma sent envoys to greet Cortez, just after he landed in Vera Cruz, Cortez felt it necessary to brag about the wealth and power of his emperor, Charles V: "My emperor is so wealthy that he eats all his meals off gold plates, with a different plate for each serving." "Our ruler," replied the Aztec emissaries, "uses a different spoon for each bite he takes!" The spoons were, of course, corn tortillas. All over Mexico, corn tortillas remain a staple accompaniment to any meal. You can use them to pick up bites of food, or for pushers to help load your spoon or fork. Soaked in sauce and rolled around meat, vegetables, or cheese, they become enchiladas.

Flat or Sonoran-style enchiladas, however, are a completely different dish. They are small, flat cakes of masa or corn dough, mixed with red chile, fried, and served under a red sauce. They have been around the Pimería for a long

time. Many of my Mexicano friends in their fifties and older never encountered the rolled enchiladas until they grew up and started eating in restaurants.
The flat ones were all they had at home. Nowadays, these regional enchiladas
can be found in many Southern Arizona restaurants.

And speaking of restaurants, have you ever noticed that so many dishes in
Mexican restaurants combine red sauce, white sour cream, and green chopped
lettuce? That's no accident, of course—those are the colors of the Mexican flag
(*la bandera*). In fact, some restaurants offer dishes in "bandera style"—with
both red and green chile sauce and sour cream. And don't forget *almendrado*,
that wonderful almond-flavored dessert, which comes in the same colors. Food
can be a statement of cultural identity in more ways than one.

But back to tortillas. Rolled or folded around just about anything, and fried
crisp or not, they become tacos. Tostadas are tortillas that have been fried crisp
and flat, and then loaded with various kinds of food. Or slightly less crisp tostadas
can serve as a base for fried eggs and salsa and cheese, and become *huevos rancheros*
(ranch-style eggs). If tortillas are allowed to get slightly stale and cut up into strips
or triangles, they can be very lightly fried for *chilaquiles*. Here in the Tucson area,
chilaquiles are served with red enchilada sauce and melted cheese on them. But I
have had chilaquiles elsewhere with sauteed onions, strips of green chile, eggs, and
various kinds of sauce, onions, cheese, or almost anything else mixed in. When
the tortillas get even staler, they can be cut into triangles and fried, to become
totopos or tortilla chips. And those are just some of the uses of corn tortillas.

In the Pimería Alta, corn tortillas decidedly take second place to those made
from wheat flour, an important part of Father Kino's legacy. I have already
discussed these Sonoran specialties in Chapter Three, and there is little that
remains to be said about them except that, as recently as the 1950s, they were
a strictly regional Sonoran food. Burros, burritos, and chimichangas had yet to
spread to other parts of the borderlands and Mexico.

A word should be said about the relatively recent urban phenomenon of taco
stands. These can operate out of campers or trailers, or they may occupy build-

ings. Their specialties are soft tacos and quesadillas, although they also serve *caramelos* (quesadillas with chopped-up carne asada) and similar specialties. You are usually offered a choice of corn or flour tortillas. Many of the stands provide a wide variety of things to put on your taco: sliced cucumber, pickled red onion, lime wedges, and two or three kinds of salsa. Grilled jalapeño peppers and grilled bulb onions round out the list of available goodies. Don't overlook those onions—they have been cooked over the coals until they are slightly charred on the outside and almost liquid when you bite into them. Such stands are completely safe places to eat when travelling in Sonora, as the food is cooked on the spot. I almost forgot another contemporary street goody—the Sonoran hot dog. It's a regular frankfurter, wrapped in bacon and served in a Mexican *birrote* roll. It is then embellished with salsa, mustard, ketchup, mayonnaise, guacamole, and frijoles. Great eating, but they can be a bit sloppy.

Sopas AND *Caldos*

Soups make up an important part of our regional cuisine, which has begun to appear in Tucson's restaurants over the past few decades. You may find both caldos and sopas on the menu. These words are to some extent interchangeable, but usually caldo refers to some sort of broth, while sopas have more solid ingredients. There are even sopas secas—"dry soups"—like spaghetti and rice. Here are the most common caldos and sopas:

Caldo de queso or cheese soup. This consists of beef or chicken stock, with onion, garlic, green chiles, and chunks of potato cooked in it. Just before serving, one adds the cheese, which melts in the hot soup.

Cazuela is a soup made with beef jerky or carne seca, and flavored with onions, potatos, tomatoes, and garlic.

Cocido contains beef skirt, ox tail, chorizo, and many kinds of vegetables, including pieces of corn cob and garbanzos.

Albóndigas are meatballs in a clear broth.

Sopa de tortilla is a broth containing tomato, onion, garlic, and fried tortilla strips. Slices of avocado may appear as a garnish. If the soup has chicken in it, it can be called *sopa azteca*.

Pozole isn't really thought of as a soup, even though it has a liquid base. It consists of bits of cooked pork and *nixtamal* or hominy in a broth. It is an important comfort food in many families and can be served as a main course. If you're sick in a Mexican household, you may well get fed pozole.

Frijoles seem to fit in here somewhere. They are usually pinto beans and are generally served in two ways: *de la olla* ("out of the pot") and *refritos*. Frijoles de la olla are just what you would expect: a mess of beans in their broth, seasoned with various spices. They are a wonderful, filling dish. Frijoles refritos are beans taken a step further, mashed up and fried, with cheese, or maybe a little milk added. These are the beans you commonly get in restaurants, often accompanied by rice. Not usually available in restaurants except for one or two in the Tohono O'odham Nation, are the small, traditional, local beans, or teparies (*bahui* in O'odham). These can be either white or brown, and may be purchased for cooking at some trading posts and farm outlets on the reservations.

And last but not least we come to *menudo*, a tripe and hominy soup. In Tucson this can be white or red from the chile that is cooked with it. (Red menudo seems to be a Texas import.) It is famous as a hangover cure, and many restaurants serve menudo only on weekends, at which time there is also a huge take-out business. It is usually eaten with Mexican baked birrote rolls rather than tortillas, and served with fresh cilantro, chopped green onion, lemon, and chiltepín (sometimes oregano as well) as garnishes. Probably because of its reputation as a hangover cure, menudo is one of the foods that are the subject of humor. I used to own a T-shirt showing a heavily moustached Mexicano, two bandoleros slung across his chest, menudo bowl, tequila bottle, and glass on the table in front of him, glaring at the observer. Underneath the picture was writ-

ten "*Menudo—desayuno de campeones.*" ("Menudo—Breakfast of Champions.")
A tourist once asked a friend of mine what menudo was. The answer: "Why,
Ma'm, it's just cow guts and popcorn." (Turkey is another country where tripe
stew is used to cure hangovers. The theory seems to be that it puts more stomach in your stomach at a time you need all the help you can get.)

More Goodies

And then there are tamales. (In Spanish, the singular is not tamale but tamal.)
These take us back to pre-conquest Mexico, and they are found all over the
country in a wild and exciting variety. Up here on the Arizona-Sonora border,
there are two basic kinds of tamales. I've already discussed the red Christmas
tamales in Chapter Two. But that's just the beginning.

In the summer, it's time for green corn tamales, or *tamales de elote.* For these,
you grind up the fresh corn, add shortening, perhaps add a little cottage cheese
for moisture, put a strip of green chile and a strip of cheese down the center of
each tamal, and wrap them in fresh shucks from the very corn you used. Then
you steam them, and eat. And eat. And eat.

Of course that's not all, even in this little area. There are sweet tamales,
wrapped in dry shucks and filled with refried beans and *piloncillo,* or raw
cane sugar. There are Sinaloa-style tamales, which are like red tamales with
a strip of carrot and a strip of potato added. And there are many variations
on all of these. In fact, each region in Mexico has its own particular tamales.
There are fish tamales, chicken tamales, shrimp tamales, huge tamales, and
bite-sized tamales. There are even blue tamales made of blue corn masa. In
southern Mexico, the tamales are wrapped in banana leaves. In fact I have
always wanted to take a Comprehensive Tamal Tour of our sister republic to
the south. Problem is, I haven't found anyone to push the wheelbarrow when
I get too full to move.

Inasmuch as our local diet is so strongly based on beef, you would think that the Pimería Alta would provide fairly slim pickings for vegetarians. Actually, this is not the case, especially if you can include cheese in your diet. *Chiles rellenos* (stuffed chiles) are available at most Mexican restaurants; they are green chiles stuffed with cheese and fried in batter. *Calabacitas* are zucchinis or zucchini-like squash. When sauteed with green chiles, onions, and perhaps a little mint, they make a wonderful meal. There is a local squash sometimes called "Papago pumpkin," which can be picked when it's lightbulb-sized and treated like a calabacita, or allowed to grow very large and cooked like a winter squash, often with milk and sugar.

Green chiles, by the way, are picked before they ripen and turn red. After that, surprisingly enough, they are called red chiles. Our common chiles in this area are the long, fairly thin fruits called "Hatch chiles" or "Anaheim chiles." But there are other kinds of chiles, even in mainstream supermarkets. Poblanos, named after the state of Puebla, to the south and east of Mexico City, are the fat, green ones you commonly find. When dried, they turn a dark red and are called *pasillas* or *anchos*. *Serranos* are the little green ones about two or three inches long. They are often used to warm up guacamole and raw salsa or salsa cruda. Jalapeños may be purchased fresh or pickled in jars or tins. Chipotles (a good Aztec word, that) are smoked jalapeños, with a wonderful, smoky flavor of their own. They usually come in tins as well.

BREAD AND BAKERIES

Mexican breads come in a wide and delicious variety. In part they are a legacy of strong nineteenth-century connections between Mexico and France. In addition to the Day of the Dead bread mentioned in Chapter Two, bakeries produce a wide variety of breads and cookies. Oh, those cookies! Each has its own name: *orejas, huaraches, banderas, cochinitos, cuernitos* ("ears," "sandals," "flags," "little pigs," "little horns"), and each has its own taste. Hard to resist. Many bakeries are attached to tortilla factories. Look them up in the Yellow Pages.

DRINKS

After all this talk about food, I'm thirsty. One traditional way to take care of that in Mexican neighborhoods is with snow cones—*raspados* in standard Spanish. (For some reason, in the Tucson area they are also called *cimarronas*, which also means "female mountain sheep. Don't ask me why.) An increasing number of Mexican restaurants also serve traditional soft drinks. Here's a sample:

Jamaica is made of hibiscus leaves that have been boiled in water, with plenty of sugar added.

Horchata is made of ground-up rice, with cinnamon and sugar, and maybe some almond flavoring.

Tamarindo comes from the seedpods of the tamarind tree.

Tesgüino is flavored with pineapple.

These are the most common ones ... but if you go to a Mexican neighborhood fiesta and see a booth sporting huge glass jars of different colored liquids, don't be afraid to go up and try.

And finally, there's *mezcal*, the distilled juice of the agave. Contrary to popular belief, agaves are succulents, not cacti. Tequila is a kind of mezcal, but to be called tequila, it must be from a special variety of agave, and come from a small area in and near the state of Jalisco. Mezcal can be made anywhere, and in fact is made in Sonora. (It used to be made in Arizona as well, during Prohibition. In the Santa Cruz Valley, moonshiners made mezcal; north of the valley, it was whiskey.)

Sonoran mezcal is often known as *bacanora* after a mountain town where it is famously made. Appropriately enough, the Bacanora plaza is decorated with huge iron sculptures of mature agave plants. But you can find it all over Sonora. There is at least one legitimate, commercial brand that sometimes shows up in Mexican liquor stores, but mostly bacanora is available in refilled bottles from the folks who make it. In other words, it's real Sonoran "white lightning." In quality it varies from a lovely smooth, slightly smoky tipple to something that will burn the guts out of a Zippo lighter. As I write this, negotiations are under way to import a truly excellent Sonoran mezcal, called "Cielo Rojo." Let's hope they prosper.

Mezcal is drunk with much the same salt-and-lime ritual that accompanies tequila, or it can have a chaser of tomato-and-chile-based Sangrita, or it can just be guzzled down neat. As the old Mexican proverb says: *Para todo mal, mezcal; y para todo bien también.* (Mezcal for all evils, and for everything good as well.)

One excellent source of traditional Tucson-area recipes is *Special Mexican Dishes: Simple and Easy to Prepare*, by Amalia Ruiz Clark. *Cocina Sonorense*, published in several editions in Hermosillo, Sonora by the Instituto Sonorense de Cultura, abounds in fine regional recipes as well. For an overview of traditional Mexican cuisine, my personal old standbys are *The Cuisines of Mexico* by Diana Kennedy and *Authentic Mexican: Regional Cooking from the Heart of Mexico* by Rick Bayless and Deann Groen Bayless.

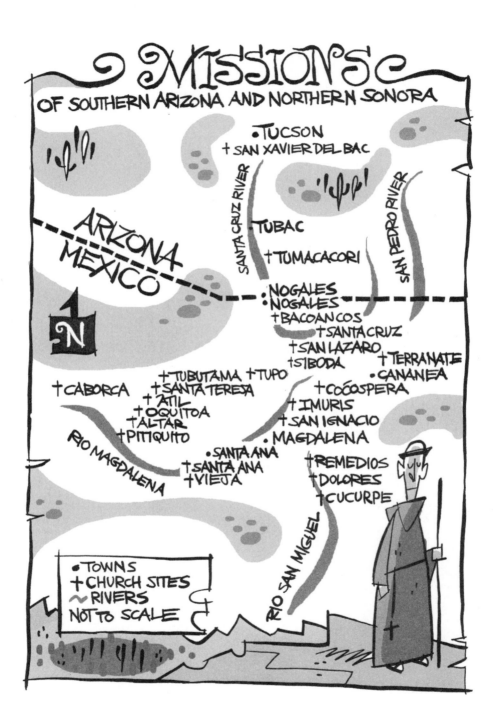

But We Can't Stop Now

NOW THAT THIS BOOK'S WRITTEN AND ON ITS WAY, it's time for another trip through the Pimería Alta. I'll invite my wife, Loma; my editor, Susan Lowell; and her publisher husband, Ross Humphreys. All three have been intimately involved in getting the book done, so it's fitting that we travel together. Let's say it's late September. The heat is beginning to drop, the rains are pretty much over, and it looks like a fine day for traveling. After picking Ross and Susan up at Rio Nuevo west of downtown Tucson, we drive over to Mission Road and head south. Just to our left is the site of Mission San Agustín, built to serve the villagers of Schuk Shon. Those buildings are gone now, scraped away to create a landfill, but the site of the old Mission Garden has been revived and is being planted with descendants of fruit trees that Father Kino and his successors brought into the Pimería. To our right is Sentinel Peak, now better known as "A" Mountain.

At some point we swing west to I-19, crossing the Santa Cruz River, that deep, dry ditch. It's not always dry, though. Someone remarks that it flowed a couple of times last summer after good storms in the Santa Ritas, and someone else reminds us that back in 1983, it was brimful of angry water, effectively cutting off Tucson's West Side for a day and washing out a couple of bridges. Not a good condition for the survival of the sensitive sand trout!

And so we go on south, past the huge mine dumps to the west, which remind us that mineral extraction has been a constant activity in southern Arizona for hundreds of years. Past the Titan Missile silo from the Cold War, which has now joined old cavalry posts and the Presidio of Tucson on our list of now-harmless historic military installations. Through the middle of Green Valley, which didn't exist at all when I arrived in Arizona in the 1950s. We finally arrive at our first stop, Tumacácori National Historic Park. We might as well leave the highway at Tubac, also the site of a Spanish presidio, and drive up the Santa Cruz Valley on the frontage road, enjoying the rural scene.

We're on our way into Sonora, so we don't spend a lot of time in Tumacácori. We greet old friends in the office, enjoy the recently redone museum, browse through the bookstore (all four of us are addicts!), and check to see how Father Kino's orchard is doing. This latter is a truly wonderful achievement, which inspired the Mission Garden project in Tucson. It is mentioned in greater detail in Chapter Three. It represents the work of Jesús García, a young ethnobotanist who created the orchard, who hails from our destination, Magdalena de Kino, and who has a deep-seated love affair with Sonora, its people, and its plants. It's too early in the project to sample any fruit, but in time ....

Refreshed and enthusiastic, we climb into the car again and head south. In the mountains to our right as we travel is the wild chiltepín preserve. Lurking in those same mountains are a lot of treasures and lost mines that never existed: the Lost Mine and the Bells of Tumacácori, the Lost Virgin of Guadalupe Mine, the Lost Ópata Mine, the Treasure and Bells of Guevavi, the Lost Mine of the Bats, and even a Tumacácori version of the Mine with the Iron Door, which most stories place in the Catalina Mountains. But reality beckons, and so we go on to Nogales, top off with gasoline, make sure we all have our passports, and enter Sonora. This time we'll take the truck crossing at Mariposa, avoid the city by way of the toll road, and join International Highway 15 south of Nogales.

Our first stop might be a brief one at a cluster of chapels along the right side of the road, just before the turnoff to the right that would take us to

Sáric and Arizonac. These chapels are dedicated to La Santa Muerte—Holy Death—and I want to see what changes have taken place in the physical manifestation of this rapidly growing devotion, which exists completely outside the Roman Catholic Church. There's a chance that there will be more chapels than when I came by the last time. Back on the highway, we discuss the road west to Arizona, the place that gave its name to our state, but decide that we just don't have time for that detour. So we truck on down the road to the Mexican Customs and Immigration stop at Kilometer 21.

Visas obtained (we don't need car permits this close to the border), we push on southward. We pass through Cibuta (which comes from an O'odham word meaning "quail's topknot" and was the site of a battle between the Constitutionalists and Pancho Villa in 1913) and head on south to Ímuris. There are interesting roadside chapels and death markers along the way, and if we had newcomers with us, we would have stopped for some photographs, but we're getting a bit hungry by now.

At Ímuris, we stop for quesadillas at one of a number of roadside stands. It isn't the law, but it sure is the custom, in this town where Father Kino established a mission, and which occasionally bills itself as "the Cheese Capital of Sonora." The kind of cheese one gets here is queso cocido or "cooked cheese," perfect for making—guess what? Quesadillas! There are several *topes* or speed humps on the highway through town, and men and women stand by them selling packages of queso cocido and tortillas to passersby. We usually get this sort of thing on the way home, so as to keep the cheese cool. (As usual, we see one or two cars of the Policía Federal de Caminos, or Federal Highway Police. I sometimes tell visitors that they are there to arrest anyone who doesn't stop and buy quesadillas. Not true, of course, and I don't try to make it stick.)

Actually we turn off the highway at the end of the mesa, just before the bus station on the right. (That's another good place for snacks, including green corn tamales as well as quesadillas.) We wind back to the main plaza of the town and then take an unmarked jog to the left and go down off the mesa, cross the river, and find ourselves on the back road to Magdalena. This road, paved in places, dirt in others, takes us on the west side of the Río Magdalena through a rich agricultural landscape. Quince orchards, crops of various kinds (including marigolds for sale on the upcoming Day of the Dead), the small towns of La Mesa and Terrenate ... we are immersed in traditional, rural Sonora. If we are traveling on a weekend, and it is very late in September, we may see little groups of pilgrims, walking towards Magdalena to pay their respects to San Francisco. We may have seen them earlier, on Highway 15, and may have also seen the temporary tents and stands set up to care for these ritual walkers. For more than a week before October 4, the entire road from Nogales to Magdalena becomes a Sacred Way, dedicated to the pilgrims and to the people who in their turn serve the saint by facilitating the walkers. I have made that walk, and I felt lifted and buoyed along on a tide of understanding and good will.

At the village of Terrenate the road swings east and crosses the river. Just past the crossing is an old brick warehouse and railroad stop, reminder of the days when foreign capital financed commercial farming ventures in northern Sonora. Painted on the side of the building is the word "PIERSON." This was once the Pierson flour mill, established in the late nineteenth century by J. E. Pierson, of a long-standing family of French immigrants. A later Pierson was a famous music teacher in Mexico City, and gave voice lessons to Jorge Negrete, perhaps the greatest *ranchera* singer of twentieth-century Mexico.

Just past the warehouse, to the west of the road, is a small rocky outcrop with some prehistoric petroglyphs—rock art, made by earlier desert people. But watch for snakes if you clamber around—they haven't gone to sleep for the winter yet.

The dirt road swings to the left, onto a low mesa, and all of a sudden we are in the village of San Ignacio, passing the cemetery. We stop for a short visit to the church, which was built by Franciscans in the late eighteenth century, and contains two statues—Santa Lucía (originally meant to represent Maria la Magdalena) and San José Oriol—that were once in the chapel where Father Kino was buried. Then on to Magdalena. We'll go back to the main road, leaving the back road to the walking pilgrims. In Magdalena we drive directly to the Plaza Monumental, which was built in the 1960s to provide a suitable setting for the bones of Father Kino.

And sure enough, there he is, under a low open-walled, domed structure. Inside the dome we see the murals of Kino's arrival and exploits, including a list of all his Pimería missions, the work of Caborcan artist Nereo de la Peña. The dome is remarkable for one other thing—it makes a perfect sounding board, so that a guide talking in a low voice on one side of Kino's grave may be heard easily by everyone standing around. Peering through one of four glassed-in windows, we look down to the original chapel floor, and see Father Kino, at rest in the land where he worked so long and hard. Flanking him are two small clusters of bones—those of Franciscans who had been buried elsewhere and reburied near Kino. (They are NOT the bones of Father Kino's faithful dog, as some folks have told me!)

And, speaking of bones, once in the 1970s I saw an O'odham family at the Kino gravesite, looking quietly down through the window at the remains of the great missionary. There was an older couple and a teenaged young man and woman. I noticed that the young man was muttering something. Like a good snoopy folklorist, I walked up to see if I could hear what the prayer or incantation was. He was saying, "The toe bone's connected to the foot bone, and the foot bone's connected to the ankle bone, and the ankle bone's ..." I crept away.

We stroll across the plaza to the church, entering the San Francisco chapel from the side. The huge crowds of pilgrims haven't yet arrived, so we are able to enter without a long wait. In a couple of days the lines will stretch through the plaza arcade to the street and involve a wait of a couple of hours. Walkers, however, go to the front of the line by long-standing custom. Inside the chapel, people are filing past San Francisco's recumbent statue, touching it on the feet, knees, and hands, lifting the statue's head, and kissing it on the cheeks or lips. For the last couple of years, the racks for candles have been moved outside near the entrance door to the chapel, so the interior is appreciably cooler than it used to be.

Obligations fulfilled, we are on the town, as all the other pilgrims will be over the next several days. Many booths are set up around both plazas, and we walk around, greeting old friends and selecting a good place to eat. We see and visit with members of the León family, who paint reverse glass frames for holy pictures, with various sellers of medicinal herbs, with a peripatetic hat sales-man, who carries his stock in one hand—handmade straw hats woven up in the Sierra and blocked at a store in Hermosillo.

After lunch, which we eat at one of the stands in or near the smaller plaza, we sit for a while and listen to the various bands that have come to town to entertain the pilgrims. From where we sit we can see two brass bands from the neighboring state of Sinaloa, one costumed mariachi, and a norteño group with button accordion, twelve-stringed bajo sexto, and a small, stand-up bass called a *tololoche*. There's also a loudspeaker somewhere, playing something else, and the total effect is festive if not particularly soothing.

But it's time to be heading home, and we pile in the car and turn its nose north towards the border. However, there are still a few stops on the way. The first of these is before we hit the International Highway, in the village of Tasí-curi, which is the turnoff for San Ignacio. (*Tasicuri*, by the way, is an ancient O'odham word, no longer used, for "javelina." Some scholars have speculated that this once represented the northernmost range of these wild peccaries, who now roam freely through southern Arizona.)

Tasícuri is also well equipped with stands selling nuts, chiltepines, queso cocido, and the thinnest flour tortillas I personally have ever encountered. (For dried chiles, it might be best to stop on the road just south of Magdalena.) We stop and buy a few dozen tortillas and perhaps some cheese, then drive on to the highway and Ímuris. Passing through Ímuris, we note a couple of roadside mural paintings of the Virgin of Guadalupe, done by Epifanio Molina and, later, by his son Sergio. Their work is to be seen all along the roads and highways in this part of Sonora. Just before we reach Cibuta, we see on the right-hand side another Guadalupana, one of two done by Miguel Romero on this stretch of the road. He painted in a totally different style than the Moli-nas, using black outlines in an almost cartoonish manner. This painted slab also marks the entrance to a small ranch, which displays a hand-lettered sign proclaiming "Hay Leña" and "Hay Queso." ("We have firewood" and "We have cheese.") The firewood doesn't tempt us on this warm late September day, but the cheese should. Leaving the car, we are ushered into the cheese-making kitchen (the work happens here in the mornings, at about 9 a.m.), where we have the opportunity to buy more tortillas, queso cocido, and the harder, saltier queso ranchero or queso regional.

Passing through Cibuta, we take the opportunity to buy yet more cheese— queso Chihuahua or queso *menonita*—Chihuahua or Mennonite cheese, which has been trucked from farms near Nuevo Casas Grandes, Chihuahua, over Highway 2, which joins our road in Ímuris. It is an aged cheese, entirely different from its Sonoran cousins, and it makes good eating melted, fried, or as is.

At last we turn our noses towards the barn, wait in line to cross the border, and drive back to Tucson; tired, full, happy, and having reconnected with several hundred years of history in one lovely day.

Afterword

LOOKING AT THINGS ONE WAY, all I really need to say at this point is "That's it, folks." I've introduced you to some stories and ideas concerning this border country—this Pimería Alta—that I love. And perhaps that's enough. But I was trained as a folklorist, and folklorists aren't simply accumulators and retellers of stories or facts. We have been taught to look for patterns, and I can see some interesting patterns in this place of ours.

In the first place, even though I have mentioned many things that happened in the past, the book as a whole is very much in the present tense. The past is only brought in to explain the living cultural world around us. Every one of the stories I have passed on has a relevance for the here and now, and should serve to connect us to that reality more firmly. In the second place, even though I've been writing about four separate and distinct cultural traditions—Mexican, Yaqui, O'odham, and Anglo-American—those traditions do not exist in sealed compartments. We live next to each other, we rub shoulders with each other. We borrow or reject each other's ideas and possessions. And sometimes we reinterpret each other's stuff so as to make it more familiar.

One good example of this took place among the Anglo Americans living in the Casa Grande area. Apparently they had heard stories about the Children's Shrine mentioned in Chapter Four, and some had visited that sacred site of the Tohono O'odham. But the retellings of that story that found their way into newspapers and magazines differed in several interesting ways from the O'odham story. In the first place, the impending disaster was not a flood but a drought. In the second place, the number of children sacrificed was three rather than four. Simple but revealing changes.

The Tohono O'odham lived in and with a desert. Drought was—and is—a normal condition, and the Desert People had a strategy for coping with severe drought: they would visit their relatives along the rivers until conditions changed. Floods, on the other hand, were devastating, destructive phenomena to be feared. It was quite the opposite for the Anglo farmers who arrived in this country later on. And while four is the significant O'odham number, three is the "magic number" for those who are European-descended. Three strikes and you're out, three guesses, the Holy Trinity—the number three permeates our culture on every possible level. So as the story of the Flood Children moved from one culture to another, it was modified so as to be more meaningful in its new home ... even though it still bore the label of "Papago legend." (I describe this process of cultural adaptation of stories in greater detail in Chapter Five of *A Shared Space: Folklife in the Arizona-Sonora Borderlands*.)

One last thought: the title of this book is *A Border Runs Through It*. And so it does. But we have crossed many borders in our travels: in and out of Pascua Yaqui and Tohono O'odham Nations, through national parks and forests, even across several centuries. All are important, to be sure, and at the same time irrelevant. We have illuminated the present by examining the past, we have listened to new words, and tasted many foods. And we have found that a unified regional culture spreads over all these political and bureaucratic divisions, split into nation states, sovereign nations, and administrative jurisdictions, but uniting them into something else, something real, that we call the Pimería Alta.

The stories and topics in this book aren't the only ones that are connected with this place, of course. I have left out the detailed descriptions of visual arts and music that make up a great part of my book, *Hecho a Mano: The Traditional Arts of Tucson's Mexican American Community.* I also wrote in greater detail concerning the traditional beliefs and religion of the Pimería Alta in *Beliefs and Holy Places: A Spiritual Geography of the Pimería Alta.* And there are always more details to be filled in, and new details and even whole stories, to be discovered. But for now this should serve as a road map or treasure chart to many of the beliefs, stories, and practices that make this Pimería of ours such a special place. Enjoy it: there's not another place just like it!

Ackowledgments

THIS BOOK IS THE DISTILLATION OF WELL over forty years of learning, listening, and looking in the Pimería Alta. I am obviously indebted to many people: fellow scholars past and present, folks who told me their stories and shared information with me—travel companions, mentors, and students. The list could be expanded to include practically everyone I've talked with since 1958, for folklorists are notorious "kiss-and-tell" types. However, I've already told most of those names in my previous books and articles. You know who you are, and are aware that this book rests entirely on your willingness to share your knowledge with me.

The folks I worked with at KUAT-TV added their expertise and enthusiasm to the project. They were, in alphabetical order, Hector Gonzales, Teresa Jones, Bob Lindberg, Jacobo Ramírez, and Martín Rubio. Good friends all, they joined in a truly collaborative effort to highlight our regional culture.

The relatively short list that follows comprises the great constants in my learning curve, plus a few others: Bernard Fontana, Alfredo Gonzales, Francisco Javier Manzo T., and Richard Morales have been my major traveling companions and mentors. My wife Loma and children Kelly and David have put up with a lot of repeated talk and stories. My editor Susan Lowell Humphreys, and publisher Ross Humphreys have provided encouragement, hard work, and good advice. Jim Turner and Edith Lowell helped with some of the final details. "Fitz" came to the project late in the game but has done wonders in setting the right visual tone. I thank you all.

Bibliography

Bahr, Donald, Juan Smith, William Smith Allison, and Julian Hayden. *The Short, Swift Time of Gods on Earth*. Berkeley and Los Angeles: The University of California Press, 1994. This gives us a version of the complete Akimul O'odham creation narrative, collected in 1935.

Barnes, Will C. *Arizona Place Names*. Originally printed in 1935. Tucson: University of Arizona Press, 1935.

Bayless, Rick, and Deann Groen Bayless. *Authentic Mexican: Regional Cooking from the Heart of Mexico*. New York: William Morrow and Company, 1987. An overview and personal standby for traditional Mexican cuisine.

Camou Healy, Ernesto, and Alicia Hinojosa. *Cocina Sonorense, Quinta Edición*. Hermosillo: Instituto Sonorense de Cultura, 2006. Published in several editions, it abounds in fine regional recipes.

Carmony, Neil B. *Onza! The Hunt for a Legendary Cat*. Silver City, NM: High-Lonesome Books, 1995.

Clark, Amalia Ruiz. *Special Mexican Dishes: Simple and Easy to Prepare*. Tucson: Roadrunner Technical Publications, 1977. This is an excellent source of traditional Tucson-area recipes.

Dadera, Don. *In Search of Jesús García*. Payson, AZ: Prickly Pear Press, 1989. Dadera tells the story of Jesús García in detail and with wonderful old photographs.

Flores, Carlotta. *El Charro Café: The Tastes and Traditions of Tucson*. Tucson: Fisher Books, 1998.

Fontana, Bernard L. "Biography of a Desert Church: The Story of Mission San Xavier del Bac," *The Smoke Signal*, no. 3, Tucson: Tucson Corral of the Westerners, 1961.

————. *A Gift of Angels: The Art of Mission San Xavier*. Tucson: University of Arizona Press, 2010.

————, photographs by John P. Schaefer. *Of Earth and Little Rain*. Flagstaff: Northland Press, 1981. This is an excellent look at the Tohono O'odham as they were in the late 20th century.

Garate, Donald T. "Arizonac: a Twentieth-Century Myth," *Journal of Arizona History*, v. 46, no. 2. Tucson: Arizona Historical Society, 2005.

————. "Who Named Arizona? The Basque Connection." *Journal of Arizona History* v. 40, no.1. Tucson: Arizona Historical Society, 1999.

Granger, Byrd Howell. *Arizona's Names (X Marks the Place)*. Scottsdale, AZ: The Falconer Publishing Company, 1983.

————. *A Motif Index for Lost Mines and Treasures Applied to Redaction of Arizona Legends, and to Lost Mine and Buried Treasure Legends Exterior to Arizona*. Tucson: University of Arizona Press, 1977.

————. *Will C. Barnes' Arizona Place Names, Revised and Enlarged by Byrd H. Granger*. Tucson: University of Arizona Press, 1960.

Griffith, James S. *Beliefs and Holy Places: A Spiritual Geography of the Pimería Alta*. Tucson: University of Arizona Press, 1992. The corua is discussed more fully in Chapter 2.

————. *Folk Saints of the Borderlands: Victims, Bandits, and Healers*. Tucson: Rio Nuevo Publishers, 2003.

————. *Hecho a Mano: The Traditional Arts of Tucson's Mexican American Community*. Tucson: University of Arizona Press, 2000. More discussion, and illustrations, of the Mexican American street art may be found here.

————. *A Shared Space: Folklife in the Arizona-Sonora Borderlands*. Logan: Utah State University Press, 1995. See Chapter 5 for the process of cultural adaptation of stories in greater detail. See Chapter 7 for more about the horse race described in the corrido, "El Moro de Cumpas."

————. *Southern Arizona Folk Arts*. Tucson: University of Arizona Press, 1988.

————. "Voices from Inside a Black Snake, Religious Monuments of Sonora's Highways." *The Journal of the Southwest*, vol. 47, no. 2 (Summer 2005).

————. "Voices from Inside a Black Snake, Part II: Sonoran Roadside Capillas." *The Journal of the Southwest*, vol. 48, no. 3 (Autumn, 2006). Information on Sonora's roadside religious monuments.

Griffith, Jim, and Francisco Javier Manzo Taylor. *The Face of Christ in Sonora*. Tucson: Rio Nuevo Publishers, 2007.

Kennedy, Diana. *The Cuisines of Mexico*. New York: Harper and Row, 1972. A general overview of traditional Mexican cuisine, an old standby.

Leddy, Betty. "La Llorona in Southern Arizona." *Western Folklore*, vol. 7, 1948.

————. "La Llorona Again." *Western Folklore*, vol. 9, 1949.

Nabhan, Gary Paul. *The Desert Smells Like Rain: A Naturalist in Papago Indian Country*. San Francisco: North Point Press, 1982. This book approaches the Tohono O'odham (formerly known as Papago) in terms of their relationship to their desert land.

————. *Gathering the Desert*. Tucson: University of Arizona Press, 1985. A good introduction to ancient wild food plants.

Officer, James E., Mardith Schuetz-Miller, and Bernard L. Fontana, eds. *The Pimería Alta: Missions and More*. Tucson: The Southwest Mission Research Center, 1996.

Olvera, Jorge H. *Finding Father Kino: The Discovery of the Remains of Father Eusebio Kino, S.J., 1965–1966*. Tucson: Southwest Mission Research Center, Inc., 1998.

Painter, Muriel Thayer. *With Good Heart: Yaqui Beliefs and Ceremonies in Pascua Village*. Tucson: University of Arizona Press, 1986.

————. *A Yaqui Easter*. Tucson: University of Arizona Press, 1983. I urge all interested readers to get a copy of this 40-page booklet.

Polzer, Charles W., S.J. *Kino: A Legacy: His Life, His Works, His Missions, His Monuments*. Tucson: The Jesuit Fathers of Southern Arizona, 1998.

————. "Legends of Lost Missions and Mines." *The Smoke Signal*, vol. 18. Tucson: Tucson Corral of the Westerners, 1968.

Probert, Thomas. *Lost Mines and Buried Treasures of the West: Bibliography and Place Names—from Kansas West to California, Oregon, Washington, and Mexico.* Berkeley: University of California Press, 1977.

Redford, Benjamin. *Tracking the Chupacabras: The Vampire Beast in Fact, Fiction, and Folklore.* Albuquerque: The University of New Mexico Press, 2011.

Rhodes, Eugene Manlove. *The Trusty Knaves.* Lincoln: University of Nebraska Press, 1988. "Cowboy Chronicler" Rhodes drew from his life in 1880s New Mexico to write this acclaimed 1930s novel.

Roach, Joyce Gibson. "The Legends of El Tejano, the Texan Who Never Was." *Western Folklore*, vol. 27, no. 1, January 1968, pp. 33-42. This is a good introduction to El Tejano.

Santamaria, Francisco J. *Diccionario de Mejicanismos.* Méjico: Editorial Porrua, S.A., 1978.

Saxton, Dean, and Lucille Saxton. *O'otham Hoho'ok A'agitha: Legends and Lore of the Papago and Pima Indians.* Tucson: University of Arizona Press, 1973. An excellent introduction to Tohono O'odham oral literature.

Seibold, Doris. "Folk Tales from the Patagonia Area, Santa Cruz County, Arizona." *University of Arizona General Bulletin*, no. 13. Tucson: University of Arizona, 1949.

Sherbrooke, Wade C. *Introduction to Horned Lizards of North America.* Berkeley: University of California Press, 2003.

Spicer, Edward H. *The Yaquis: A Cultural History.* Tucson: University of Arizona Press, 1980.

Tucson Pima Arts Council. *Murals: Guide to Murals in Tucson.* Tucson: Tucson Pima Arts Council, 1993. It should still be available in many libraries, and also online: http://parentseyes.arizona.edu/folkarts/murals.html.

Wasley, William W. "Ravaged Ruins: The Destruction of Our Cultural Heritage." *The Smoke Signal,* vol. 18, Tucson: Tucson Corral of the Westerners, 1968.

Index

"A" Mountain, 7, 105

Akimel O'odham, 78

Altar, 63

Altar Valley, 10, 60, 66, 86

Apaches, 57, 60, 61

Átil, 59

Baboquivari Peak, 10, 77, 79

Bacanora, 101

barrios, 9–10; street art, 37–41

Barrio Volvo, 9

Barrio Sobaco, 10

Borderlands Theater, 45

breads, 100

burros, 65–67

Caborca, 59, 62–63

caldos, 97–98

capirotada, 46

carabunco, 86

carne asada, 66, 67

carne seca, 67

Casa Cordova, La, 44

cascarones, 47–48

Cat Mountain, 12

champurrada, see "Christmas"

chapayekas, see "Yaquis"

Children's Shrine, see "shrines"

chiles, 100

chiles rellenos, 100

chiltepines, 94

chimichanga, 65

Christmas, 43–46; champurrada, 45; Las Pastorela, 44, 45–46; Las Posadas, 44–45

chupacabras, 86–87

Cinco de Mayo, el, 41–42

Cocóspera, 59, 60

cookies, 100

corridos, 34–36

Corua, La, 84, 86

Crabb, Henry Alexander, 63

Cucurpe, 3

Cumpas, 34–35

death markers, see "shrines"

Día de Guadalupe, el, 43

Día de los Muertos, el, 46–47; pan de muerto, 47

Día de los Reyes, el, 46

Día de San Juan, 27

Dieciseis de Septiembre, 41

Diego, Juan, 39, 43

Dolores, 59

drinks, 101; horchata, 101; jamaica, 101; mezcal, 101–102; raspados, 101; tamarindo, 101; tesgüino, 101

Easter, see "Yaquis"

fariseos, see "Yaquis"

Fiesta de los Vaqueros, la, 42

Flood Children, 80–81

frijoles, 98

García, Jesús, 35–36

García Yáñez, Jesús (ethnobotanist), 64, 106

graffiti, 38–39

Hermosillo, 54, 56, 102

Ho'ok, 79–80

horned lizards, 29

I'itoi, 77, 79–81

Ímuris, 59, 66, 107, 110, 111

Jesuit Order, 16, 21, 51, 54, 59, 70

Juneteenth, 43

Kino, Eusebio Francisco, 3, 16, 19, 51–54, 55, 59–67; missions, 16, 59–67; orchard, 64

Lake Elmira, 28

Lent, see "Yaquis"

Llorona, La, 30–31

lost mines, 67–72; Lost Ópata Mine, 69, 106; Lost Virgin of Guadalupe Mine, 68, 70–71, 106; Mine with the Iron Door, 72, 106

lost treasure, 67–72

Lost Virgin of Guadalupe Mine, see "lost mines"

low riders, 40

maehto, see "Yaquis"

Magdalena, 52–58; fiesta, 58; pilgrimage, 56–58

mariachis, 36
matachines, see "Yaquis"
menudo, 98–99
Mexican Independence
   Day, see "Dieciseis de
   Septiembre"
Mine with the Iron Door,
   see "lost mines"
monsoon, 26–27
Mount Hopkins, 9
Mount Wrightson, 9
murals, 17, 39–40
nacimiento, 43–44
Nacozari, 35
ñehbig, 79, 84
Nogales, 56, 57, 74–75,
   106, 108
Olizarra, Joaquín, 61
onza, 87–88
Ópata 69
Oquitoa, 47, 60–61
organ pipe cactus, see
   "pitahaya"
pachucos, 10
pajareros, 83
pan de muerto, see "Día de
   los Muertos, el"
pascolas, see "Yaquis"
Pastorela, Las, see
   "Christmas"
Pato de Gallo, 37
pelicannon, 89
Picacho Peak, 9, 10, 12
piñatas, 47–48

pitahaya, 93–94
Pitiquito, 59, 62
Posadas, Las, see
   "Christmas"
Pozo Verde, 79–80
pozole, 98
Presidio de Tucson, 42
quesadillas, 65, 66, 97, 107
queso, 66–67, 107
Roach, Joyce Gibson, 12
saguaro, 93–94
San Francisco Xavier, 54–
   58, 60, 73, 83, 108–109
San Ignacio, 60, 108, 110
San Ramón Shrine, see
   "shrines"
San Xavier del Bac, 16–20
Sand People, 78
sand trout, 28–29
Santa Muerte, la, 75, 107
Santa Rosa, 80
santo himdag, 82
Sawtooth Mountains, 10
Se'e'e, 81
shrines; capillita, 73;
   Children's Shrine, 80–81;
   death markers, 72–73;
   front yard, 38; nicho, 73;
   roadside 74–75; rock-
   pile, 73; San Ramón
   Shrine, 74; El Tiradito,
   13–15
Sierra Madre, 11, 87
sonim, see "Yaquis"

Sonoyta, 13, 56
sopas, 97–98
stick lizards, 88, 89
tamales, 44, 45, 99
Tejano, El, 11–13
Tena, María Luisa, 44
Tiradito, El, see "shrines"
Tohono O'odham, 5, 43,
   56, 58, 77–84
tortillas, 95–97
Tubutama, 60, 61, 72
Tucson Meet Yourself, 4-5,
   42, 81, 83–84
Tumacácori, 10, 57, 64, 68,
   69, 70–71, 83, 106
Tumacácori Mountains, 94
Virgin of Guadalupe, 22,
   39–40, 43, 44, 110
waila, 83–84
Yaquis, 20–26, 58, 86, 112,
   113; chapayekas, 22–25;
   Easter, 20–26; fariseos,
   22–25; Lent, 20–24;
   maehto, 22, 25;
   matachines, 22–24;
   pascolas, 23–25; sonim,
   23
Zaragoza, Ignacio, 41

About the Author

JIM GRIFFITH, internationally recognized folklorist and former director of the Southwest Folklore Center at the University of Arizona, has studied traditional folkways and religious expression through the American Southwest and northern Mexico for more than four decades. He also founded the annual Tucson Meet Yourself Festival. In 2011 Jim was named a National Heritage Fellow by the National Endowment for the Arts, for his contribution to the preservation and awareness of cultural heritage. He lives in Tucson, Arizona.

About the Illustrator

DAVID "FITZ" FITZSIMMONS is a cartoonist, humor columnist, and editorial writer for the *Arizona Daily Star*. His cartoons are syndicated to over 700 news outlets. A Pulitzer finalist in 1988, his award-winning cartoons have drawn fire and praise since Geronimo was a paperboy way back in 1986. He lives in Tucson, Arizona.